HANGING THE PRACTICE OF
TEACHER EDUCATION

THE

ROLE

OF

THE

KNOWLEDGE

BASE

MARLEEN C. PUGACH
HENRIETTA L. BARNES
LEONARD C. BECKUM

American Association of Colleges for Teacher Education

CHANGING THE PRACTICE OF TEACHER EDUCATION

THE

ROLE

OF

THE

KNOWLEDGE

BASE

MARLEEN C. PUGACH

HENRIETTA L. BARNES

LEONARD C. BECKUM

American Association of Colleges for Teacher Education

February 1991

This document and the projects that led to its production were supported by a grant from the Exxon Education Foundation.

The opinions, conclusions, and recommendations expressed in this monograph do not necessarily reflect the views or opinions of the American Association of Colleges for Teacher Education. The AACTE does not endorse or warrant this information. The AACTE is publishing this document to stimulate discussion, study, and experimentation among educators. The authors were encouraged to express their judgments freely. The reader must evaluate this information in light of the unique circumstances of any particular situation and must determine independently the applicability of this information thereto.

Copies of
Changing the Practice of Teacher Education:
The Role of the Knowledge Base
may be ordered from:

AACTE Publications
One Dupont Circle, Suite 610
Washington, DC 20036-1186

Single copy (prepaid) $26.00 for AACTE representatives
$30.00 for nonrepresentatives

Library of Congress Catalog Number: 91-70872

International Standard Book Number: 0-89333-080-9

CONTENTS

FOREWORD

The following chapters are a continuation of the efforts of the American Association of Colleges for Teacher Education to promote dialogue and discussion regarding the knowledge base for the beginning teacher. Taken together, they are intended to enable faculty and students to carefully consider a range of issues concerning the transformation of their teacher education programs. Indeed, an inherent purpose for this volume is to encourage faculty to consider the process of change itself as it applies to teacher education programs.

These chapters are also an outgrowth of the efforts of the Exxon Education Foundation to promote significant change in the preparation of teachers. The leadership of L. Scott Miller, while at Exxon, helped to shape a series of initiatives intended to improve dramatically the quality of teaching in the nation's schools. Mr. Miller understood the significance of teacher educators agreeing on a knowledge base for teaching and incorporating it in all facets of their programs. He encouraged the creation of the Association's Task Force on the Knowledge Base and supported the efforts of Maynard C. Reynolds and his colleagues in conceptualizing a volume of readings on what beginning teachers need to know. His sponsorship, through the Exxon Foundation, of the work that led to *Knowledge Base for the Beginning Teacher* serves as a testimonial to the commitment, wisdom, and leadership roles demonstrated by key personnel in some of the nation's leading philanthropic institutions.

Even before the slim red volume of readings appeared, in the winter of 1989, Mr. Miller was encouraging the Association to consider how *Knowledge Base for the Beginning Teacher* could be used on campuses to promote debate and discussion regarding programs that would lead to change. AACTE never intended that a particular college or university would adopt the volume "wholesale" and then attempt to incorporate every concept into its program. Clearly, that was impossible. Rather, we wanted to encourage faculty (often with groups of teachers from elementary and secondary schools) in schools, colleges, and departments of education to carefully consider the concepts that were presented in the book and then to seek ways of reconceptualizing programs to manifest the most compelling of these ideas. We expected faculty groups to identify a conception of teaching and learning consistent with their own strengths and to then use the volume to consider, in a meaningful way, the relationship of a knowledge base framework to their programs of teacher preparation.

From the inception of this project, there was the recognition that the knowledge base for teacher education differs in some important ways from the knowledge base for teaching; it must also include a serious consideration of the change process. While there exists an enormous amount of work on the process of change for schools and universities, little exists regarding the ways in which institutions or education units confront the challenge of change and actually transform programs. The work that does exist consists of descriptions of particular institutional efforts, or efforts that focus on a certain theme, e.g., Competency Based Teacher Education. At least since the mid-1980s, AACTE understood that some greater understanding of the process of change as it was attempted in schools, colleges, and departments of education was needed. This effort is essential to understand how faculty and administrators confront the necessity for change, go about the business of plotting a direction, and then transform programs to fulfill a set of expectations.

In response to this need, it was agreed that different types of institutions would have different experiences as they considered *Knowledge Base for the Beginning Teacher*. Consequently, it was determined that we would fund a small number of institutions (an urban "regional" college, a small liberal arts college, a major land-grant institution, etc.) and encourage them to document the process used in considering the concepts and ideas found in the twenty-four presentations of the KBBT* volume. We also encouraged these institutions to form clusters of other institutions, to enable a critical mass of faculty from up to a half-dozen professional education units to work together in this endeavor. The idea of a "lead institution" building a cluster of other institutions from the region and then identifying a theme, e.g., the significance of the knowledge base for preparing elementary teachers, was the idea that evolved. Seven such clusters were

---

* *In the text that follows, the 1989 AACTE publication* Knowledge Base for the Beginning Teacher *will generally be referred to as "the KBBT volume." Citations and appropriate reference listings appear in the individual chapters.*

funded with a modest amount of resources to be used to bring together faculty to consider these themes.

That we were asking institutions to both document change on their own campus while expanding the dialogue to include other institutions is typical of what is necessary when there are scarce resources to promote change. These factors need to be considered by anyone seeking to replicate this strategy or to draw inferences for their own efforts at change. Whether it was the funds provided by the Exxon Education Foundation, the stimulus provided by the KBBT volume, the identification of the seven sites by the Association's staff, the reinforcement provided by the cluster concept, or a number of other variables, the accompanying monograph is a testimony to the success of this strategy. The chapters that follow are a thoughtful compendium of the ideas that emerged from these clusters. They have been written by a talented group of authors and compiled in this volume with considerable expertise by Marleen Pugach, Henrietta Barnes, and Leonard Beckum. I believe they provide helpful insights into the process of change in higher education. Certainly, they offer perspective on the struggle of faculty to build coherent programs that are both responsive to new knowledge and to the demands of teaching in the nation's schools.

This volume also serves another important purpose, namely, to help this Association in its identification of next steps in the preparation of a revision of *Knowledge Base for the Beginning Teacher*. From the inception of this effort, it was recognized that the KBBT volume was a preliminary step by AACTE in the identification of concepts and ideas important for beginning teachers to know and be able to use. We understood that any identification of themes and topics would necessarily be incomplete. Some chapters of this monograph identify themes the authors believe were not treated in sufficient depth or with adequate attention in the KBBT volume. Clearly, one of the most compelling of these themes has to do with teaching youngsters from an expanding array of diverse backgrounds and experiences. Much more attention is needed in subsequent editions of the knowledge base volume regarding this topic in order to assist teacher educators in preparing effective teachers for our schools.

The dynamic nature of building a knowledge base for teacher education is what emerges from this volume. This dynamic interplay involves an interactive process of identifying consensus on new knowledge, codifying it in useful form, seeking its utilization by faculty and students, and verifying its utility and completeness. An important part of this process is the Association's commitment to the ongoing revision of the KBBT volume and to ensuring that contributions from this monograph and other sources enable an expansion of our professional knowledge.

DAVID G. IMIG
EXECUTIVE DIRECTOR

February 1991

PROLOGUE

WILLIAM E. GARDNER

One of the most persistent themes in the current debate over American education is the need to enhance the status of teachers and teaching in the United States. Certainly the core idea in the Carnegie Report (*A Nation Prepared: Teachers for the 21st Century*), and a central feature of several publications of the American Association of Colleges for Teacher Education and the Holmes Group, is the need to move teaching from the ranks of semiprofessions, to equip the profession with more of the attributes of law and medicine, and to enhance and empower teachers by making teaching a true profession.

To be sure, the rhetoric surrounding this "professionalizing" agenda contains a great many contradictions and confusing elements. The word "profession" is too often defined in self-serving terms. Thus, school board groups at times urge teachers to be professional, meaning that they should be less aggressive at salary negotiation time. Teacher groups, on the other hand, at times define professionalism only in terms of wage and hour benefits. Teacher educators often talk about the need to develop professional programs but do not move aggressively to provide their own programs with professional characteristics. But beyond the confusing, the contentious, and the petty, there is solid debate and very good thinking going on related to the belief that teaching is undervalued in the United States and as a vocation, its status is too low.

A burgeoning literature deals with trends and issues in this professionalizing movement. Much of this work centers on the description of potential new roles and relationships for teachers and on new school arrangements which allow both greater freedom and responsibility for those who work in schools.

The rationale for this enhanced view of teaching is rooted in the idea that the schooling process today is more important and more difficult than ever before. It is more important because knowledge in a general sense has become absolutely central to modern life. There is obvious need for better education for all children and adolescents, not just an elite; the world our young people will soon control demands more knowledgeable citizens. The schooling process is more difficult because an increasing percentage of people come to school without strong learning support systems in the home, and they are ill-equipped to participate in schools that ask them, at an early age, to compete where they cannot be successful.

The nation's school systems, then, need teachers who can work with all learners, especially at a time when the contexts of schooling are more complicated than ever before. We need professionals to do this important and difficult work.

The key characteristic of such professionals is that they possess knowledge that is distinct from the general knowledge of a lay person. Whether or not such a body of knowledge exists has been sharply debated in recent years. Education as a field of study and teaching as an applied activity have been sorely handicapped by the lack of a body of coherent and agreed upon professional knowledge. Law has its analytical case study methods, medicine has its scientific knowledge, nursing its mix of scientific and conventional wisdom, but until very recently conversations in the field of education had not reached the point where such a knowledge base could be identified. Lack of a knowledge base for education has encouraged the adoption of fads and pop solutions to major issues and has hampered the development of strong professional programs to train teachers and strong induction programs for clinical practice.

The claim that teaching lacked a knowledge base had some credence 20 years ago, but the situation has changed dramatically. In recent years there has been a small avalanche of publications dealing with the knowledge base, much of this output drawn from the process-product research efforts but much also from other fields as well. While no one is yet willing to say without equivocation that a hard core of professional knowledge has been identified and agreed upon, it is certainly clear that a valuable and rich store of information has been accumulated about the set of actions that we call teaching and that there is growing consensus on what both beginning and advanced teachers should know and be able to do.

The need to identify, codify, and test a body of knowledge for teaching was identified in the mid '80s by leadership of the American

Association of Colleges for Teacher Education. A task force was formed to suggest ways that the Association could adopt a more aggressive posture on both the identification of a knowledge base for beginning teachers and the implementation of that knowledge base in programs of teacher education. Out of this effort came *Knowledge Base for the Beginning Teacher* (KBBT), a volume designed to enunciate a clear public statement of what the knowledge base for beginners should be and to persuade some substantial proportion of the teacher-education community that these ideas are worthy of attention and should be embraced.

 The group that designed the KBBT volume recognized and acknowledged early on that the mere publication of a book on it would not solve the problem of the knowledge base, but they argued that identification and codification of the knowledge base was a necessary step if the state of teaching was to be improved. The work of collating and codifying the knowledge base should be done by those who had expertise in the various areas of knowledge. The group worked, then, on the assumption that agreement among experts (in the words of the KBBT volume, a "consensus doctorum") should be broad-based, including not only teacher educators and researchers, but policymakers and teacher practitioners as well. Indeed, the definition of content for the KBBT volume was done ultimately by a combination of researchers, teacher educators, and teacher practitioners.

 Once the KBBT volume had been published, it was clear that two steps were needed. The first was to establish a way for the knowledge base to be reviewed and critiqued with the eye toward an early revision. A new group was formed specifically charged with that task. The second step was to demonstrate how the vast landscape of information relative to the knowledge base for beginning teachers could be included in teacher-education programs. This is an enormously important and very difficult problem, and one that this volume seeks to address.

 For some time a group of institutions had been working under the aegis of grants from the Exxon Education Foundation to review the KBBT volume and to examine the ways in which the volume could be helpful in the revision of teacher education programs. Institutional groups were formed among these AACTE members, and each proceeded independently to look at aspects of the knowledge base and ways to use it productively. The basic question investigated was whether true program change could, in fact, take place based on the up-to-date and current knowledge base.

This book reports the results of these Exxon-sponsored projects as follows. Section One summarizes efforts made in these projects to conceptualize the knowledge base for teacher education programs. Although not representative of the full range of conceptual issues that need to be addressed, these efforts are informative as examples of collaborative ways to think about the redesign of teacher education programs. In Chapter 1, Barnes discusses issues to think about in recasting the knowledge base for use with prospective teachers. Next Pugach and Leake (Chapter 2) consider contextualizing the knowledge base for the preparation of teachers in a pluralistic society. In Chapter 3, Beckum and an international study group report their analysis of what knowledge successful teachers in multicultural and multilingual settings perceived to be critical. In this section's concluding chapter, Murray (Chapter 4) describes ways to conceptualize the design of the academic liberal arts major for elementary teachers.

The second section of this book discusses major challenges faced by teacher educators as they attempt to revise their programs. While also concerned with developing an adequate and appropriate knowledge base for their programs, the projects described in this section deal more directly with the process of change itself and provide examples of various strategies employed in attempting to accomplish the reform goals.

Barnes (Chapter 5) notes the difficulties of achieving change in institutions and presents some of the ways of overcoming these difficulties. Four case studies follow, each offering different strategies for addressing these issues. Pasch, Pugach, and Fox (Chapter 6) discuss the process used at the University of Wisconsin at Milwaukee, which involved creating an alternative collaborative structure for faculty interaction. In Chapter 7, Putnam discusses how faculty development might be stimulated from the outside. Barnes (Chapters 8) and Richner (Chapter 9) provide insights from the use of different implementation strategies at a large, multipurpose institution and a small liberal arts college.

These projects all had some very exciting results and deserve attention by several key groups. The primary audience should be teacher-educators faced with the challenging task of redesigning their teacher-education programs in the light of the emerging knowledge base. The leadership cadre of this group—the deans and chairpersons of colleges and departments of education—should also find this book useful, as should state officials whose work involves the content of teacher education. ■

CHANGING THE PRACTICE OF TEACHER EDUCATION

ACKNOWLEDGMENTS

This volume represents the collaborative efforts of a number of individuals who are centrally concerned with improving the practice of teacher education, and each deserves great thanks. Scott Miller, formerly of the Exxon Education Foundation, supported this work through the Knowledge Base Grant Project housed at AACTE and at the seven institutions that participated in related projects. His successor, Michael Dooley, has continued to lend his support to this ongoing effort. An edited volume depends on its contributing authors, and we have been fortunate to work with a group of authors who have willingly and skillfully shared their insights about changing the practice of teacher education and who were responsive to our editorial efforts in both time and substance.

Carol Smith, Senior Director for Professional Issues at AACTE, kept us on task by providing endless hours of organizational support, feedback on earlier versions of the chapters, and editorial assistance. She also coordinated all technical aspects of production. It is safe to say that without her support, our job as editors would have been infinitely more difficult. Much assistance was provided by AACTE staff members Kristen Van Camp, Carolyn Armstrong, and Sharon Givens.

MARLEEN PUGACH
UNIVERSITY OF WISCONSIN-MILWAUKEE

HENRIETTA BARNES
MICHIGAN STATE UNIVERSITY

LEONARD BECKUM
DUKE UNIVERSITY

TRANSFORMING

KNOWLEDGE

FOR

TEACHER

EDUCATION

RECONCEPTUALIZING THE KNOWLEDGE BASE FOR TEACHER EDUCATION

1

HENRIETTA L. BARNES

Overview.   Transforming the knowledge base for beginning teachers into curricula for teacher education is complicated because the understandings that beginning teachers need are not merely the sum of content from the different domains related to teaching. If understanding did, indeed, accrue automatically from learning about concepts and principles from different domains and then transferring that knowledge to the diverse settings where it might be used, then teacher education curricula could simply consist of courses on each of the different domains. We are learning, however, that teacher knowledge is more complex. Not only must teacher educators consider what beginning teachers need to know, they must also take into account how teachers come to understand teaching and learning within different contexts. This chapter is motivated by the conviction that teacher educators must go beyond the content presented in the KBBT volume to conceptualize programs of teacher preparation that consider both the means and the ends to be served by the program. ■

One of the most heartening features of present efforts to reform teacher education is the current serious attempt to define a knowledge base for teaching. Rooted in a respect for the complexity of teachers' work that has emerged from research on teaching over the past two decades, the need for teachers to make numerous professional judgments and decisions in the daily course of their work is now commonly acknowledged among educators. The role of knowledge in informing those judgments and decisions is less clear. That teachers need and use knowledge, even specialized knowledge, is not debated. What the nature and the sources of that knowledge are and how teachers use the knowledge they have is at the heart of what will continue to be one of the primary debates in teacher education for the next several years.

Part of the reason the debate is likely to continue lies in the fact that we, as teacher educators, have defined the knowledge base of our teacher education curricula very narrowly. And, we have failed to relate important concepts from one discipline with essential content from other fields of study within our teacher education curricula. Teaching practice, on the other hand, requires the simultaneous use of knowledge drawn from several disciplines and acquired from many sources to achieve specific purposes with particular learners.

Individually and as a group, those who educate teachers typically rely on limited sources of knowledge for creating their curricula. Frequently, these sources are constrained by their own experience as students or educators within specific disciplines that have led to strong biases in support of a particular specialty area, often to the exclusion of knowledge from other areas. Or, research-based knowledge generated from the study of specific teaching problems (e.g., how to ask higher-order questions or advance critical thinking, or how to organize and manage instruction in classrooms), is used to justify the content of the program.

The disadvantages of basing the teacher education curriculum on the cumulative interests of different specialists' views are apparent in the fragmented nature of many curricula. Such programs typically offer no conceptual frame within which teacher candidates can build a knowledge base or a coherent vision of practice, and thus are often labeled irrelevant by graduates of these programs. Criticized primarily for their failure to prepare prospective teachers for the realities of teaching subject matter and other important content to diverse youngsters in increasingly difficult settings, these programs are seen as idealistic, unrelated to practice, and, therefore, expendable. The disadvantages of basing programs solely on research are less obvious but equally serious. They stem from the unwarranted credence we afford knowledge labeled scientific, and from our failure to understand the contextualized nature of knowledge. The need to consider ends as well as means when constructing teacher education curricula adds to the difficulty of figuring out how to use that research in the service of the teacher education curriculum.

In some ways, it is counterintuitive to question the role of research knowledge in teacher education. For many years, teacher educators have been exhorted to build their programs exclusively on such knowledge. This recommendation came from the desire to gain for teachers and teacher educators the respect afforded others given the title of professional. Rhetoric during the '70s and '80s called for a codified or scientific knowledge base that would elevate the status of teachers and teacher educators as professionals. Research on teaching was seen as the logical source of such knowledge. Until recently, however, not much thought was given to the role such research could or should play in informing practice that could be deemed professional (Lampert & Clark, 1990). And, how research maps onto the local concerns of the school and community typically was not addressed.

Access to a body of scientific knowledge is one way to designate the specialized nature of a group's work and training. Teaching and teacher education, however, cannot be reduced to knowledge of this sort. The dilemma created by the pursuit of a "scientific" knowledge base to enhance teacher professionalism is that it sometimes denies the contribution that teacher wisdom can make to the definition of that knowledge base. Most often, however, the pursuit neglects to engage teachers and teacher educators in essential but value-laden conversations about the aims or ends of teaching and teacher education. If teacher education is to continue to play a major role in helping teachers construct an adequate base of knowledge for teaching, both initially and throughout their careers, it cannot avoid these questions. Because the aim of reform in teacher education is crafting a more appropriate and effective curriculum and pedagogy, conversations about that reform must go beyond either unexamined personal opinion or empirical research. Other voices and considerations as well as other sources of knowledge (e.g., craft knowledge, cultural knowledge, and beliefs and values that guide the moral and ethical dimensions of professional practice) must also be addressed.

Since knowledge is the primary justification for formal teacher education, the future of teacher education as an educational enterprise depends on how the community of teacher educators and teachers resolve this dilemma.

Examinations of the purposes and outcomes of current curricula in teacher education call attention to the need for rethinking both the depth and breadth of those curricula (Feiman-Nemser & Buchmann, 1986; Kennedy, 1987; NCRTE, 1988; Zeichner, 1981; Zimpher & Howey, 1989). Knowledge drawn from the disciplines that undergird teaching can contribute importantly to the new curricula that must be created. But programs designed to prepare individuals to begin to teach must also take into account (1) the ways in which teachers are special, (2) the sorts of understandings that make them unique, and (3) the role that initial teacher education plays in shaping those distinctive qualities. Thoughtful responses to these questions are essential to the definitional problem confronting teacher educators.

THE DILEMMA OF DEFINING THE KNOWLEDGE BASE FOR TEACHER EDUCATION

While the term *knowledge base* is now a part of discussions involving teacher education, questions involving the use of the term and what it signifies abound. The confusion in the literature stems in part from a failure to specify the meanings we bring to our various uses of the term, and in part from a failure to draw important distinctions between the various sources of knowledge that can inform teaching and the ways in which that knowledge is used. As was pointed out earlier, the term is sometimes used to refer to the base of research-generated technical knowledge that a program provides. This definition supports the view that teaching is a science and that people who have demonstrated through successful completion of coursework that they know that content are qualified to be licensed to teach. How such knowledge is used in teaching is not a primary consideration when the term is used in this way.

At other times, *knowledge base* is used to refer to an individual teacher's store of knowledge and wisdom in using that knowledge. This use of the term moves beyond equating professionalism with the passing of coursework that may include the demonstration of technical competence. Instead, the term focuses on the judgments that are made by expert teachers engaged in practice. Since not all judgments are presumably wise judgments, it suggests that special knowledge has been constructed and is used by teachers who are said to have acquired the wisdom of practice.

Still other references deal with various kinds of knowledge, for example, practical knowledge (Connelly & Clandinin, 1986; Elbaz, 1987) versus theoretical knowledge about learning or development. Sometimes, the various domains of knowledge are referred to as discrete knowledge bases. Thus one might have a base of knowledge about the teaching of particular school subjects such as English or mathematics. A few (Barnes, 1989; Cross, 1990, Valli & Tom 1988;) have emphasized the importance of knowledge frameworks as a critical feature of a knowledge base.

As these examples illustrate, the conception of the teacher's roles and images of how those roles are enacted clearly influence the knowledge priorities that various scholars advocate as appropriate teacher knowledge. Similarly, different ideas about how teacher knowledge is organized and can be made more accessible during interactive teaching also impact alternative conceptions of the knowledge base for teaching. The knowledge base for the beginning teacher then, is not a unitary concept that represents a consensus among teacher educators, nor is there agreement on how teachers most effectively acquire this knowledge base. Some promising directions are beginning to emerge, however.

Based on the view that a teacher's responsibilities require both specific and general knowledge from a number of domains that have been variously categorized, several scholars are attempting to show the interaction among otherwise discrete areas of relevant knowledge. Shulman (1987), for example, has identified those domains of knowledge that directly inform a teacher's instructional decisions and actions. Thus, he considers knowledge of subject matter, learners, curriculum, general pedagogy, content-specific pedagogy, contexts, and educational goals and values as critical components of a teacher's knowledge base. In addition, Shulman and his colleagues draw attention to the integrative nature of teacher knowledge. This work highlights the inadequacy of teaching these different but equally important areas as if they were noninteracting entities. Similarly, while the KBBT volume identifies domains of knowledge that contribute to the teacher's ability to foster learning and carry out extended professional roles, its format subtly communicates that mastery of knowledge about these domains is adequate preparation for beginning to teach and that the domains are additive rather than interactional.

If a knowledge base for teaching encompasses not only mastery of content that can inform wise judgments and actions, but also the capacity to integrate that knowledge and relate it to professional practice, then teacher education curricula must be reconceptualized. Not only must teachers have deep understandings of the subjects they will teach, the diversity of experience and cultural backgrounds that their learners will bring to the learning situation, and the contextual circumstances they will encounter, they must also have deep understandings of how these components interact and influence teaching and learning in practice. Because these factors demonstrate themselves in myriad ways in daily teaching situations, novices must become expert at examining their own practice and be capable of continuing to learn. The proposed knowledge base for teaching must be expanded to include areas that extend beyond responsibility for a single classroom of pupils. The ability to work with at-risk and special needs populations in the schools, to provide for extended interactions and involvement with parents and the community, and to contribute to the community of professional educators, thus also become important components of an acceptable knowledge framework for teacher education programs.

On the surface, research findings on teaching appear to provide a reasonable and straightforward source upon which to build teacher education. In fact, teacher education programs have traditionally operated on the assumption that knowledge about teaching, once supported by research and the collegium of scholars who contribute to the teacher education enterprise, should become the substance of coursework required for teacher certification. Despite its face validity, however, this approach to designing teacher education programs has proven inadequate as a sole basis for determining the content of teacher education. The inadequacy of limiting the curriculum in this way emphasizes the need to go beyond consideration of domains of knowledge that may contribute to a teacher's knowledge base to include consideration of what teacher educators must understand in order to prepare novices to teach.

A clear distinction needs to be made between what teachers need to know in order to foster valuable student learning (i.e., the knowledge base for teaching) and what teacher educators need to consider in order to create a curriculum that will allow novices to gain such knowledge. In this chapter, the knowledge base for teaching is defined broadly as including all of the knowledge from a variety of sources that contribute to the teacher's capacity to foster student learning and to carry out a teacher's other classroom and school-related professional responsibilities. Therefore, it includes but is not limited to technical, rational knowledge of research on teaching and learning, or discrete knowledge of learners or subject matter alone.

Like teachers, teacher educators must also be concerned about fostering learning in their students. And, like teachers, teacher educators must understand the factors that will enhance their students' ability to gain powerful and empowering knowledge. While the categories of knowledge that teacher educators must understand are similar to those of teachers (e.g., knowledge of their learners and of the particular contexts in which learning will take place), teacher educators must create opportunities in which such knowledge is learned. It is to six specific considerations surrounding the role of the knowledge base for teaching in the redesign of teacher education programs that we now turn.

CONSIDERATION ONE: THE DIFFERENCE BETWEEN TEACHING AND LEARNING TO TEACH

In discussions about teacher education, we are talking about what teachers need to know and how essential knowledge can be used to advance pupil learning. Such knowledge contains nothing about the question of how such knowledge is learned. In discussions about the knowledge base for teacher education, on the other hand, we are talking not only about outcomes of knowing and the ends to be served by such knowledge, but about what teacher educators need to know in order to help novices become professional teachers. Since learning to teach is different from teaching, teacher educators must be concerned about both the content of the teacher education program and how that program will be delivered.

For example, an important source of knowledge for teaching is the research on the effects of teacher expectations (Lampert & Clark, 1990). This material could be presented solely in a course on learning and development, it could be threaded throughout a program as one of a number of unifying concepts, or it could be addressed during clinical experiences as the phenomenon itself unfolds for the teacher education students. What is important here is that the research does not tell the teacher candidate or the teacher educator precisely what to do. The teacher educator is making judgments about such questions, however, and so must grapple with interpretations of the research given the ends of the teacher education curriculum. In other words, how one chooses to deal with knowledge for teaching in a particular program of teacher education is different from merely acknowledging that a piece of knowledge is critical for the preparation of teachers.

The limited value of empirical studies of teaching can also be considered in the broader picture of how someone learns to teach. Scholarship on learning to teach is now seen as a legitimate area of study. Distinctions between teaching and learning to teach are not as sharp as they once were because of the growing knowledge base tied to research on learning to teach (Feiman-Nemser & Buchmann, 1986; NCRTE, 1988). For example, some studies have demonstrated that the background knowledge that prospective teachers bring to their professional study may interfere with their learning of the content of a program. One research finding related to this phenomenon is that these views are not easily changed (Florio-Ruane & Lensmire, 1990). Teacher education students do not enter teaching absent conceptions of contexts, for example. But, they rarely understand that contexts are not only given, but are made by human beings, and are, therefore, changeable. Knowledge of beginners' tacit understandings is essential knowledge for teacher educators. As greater attention is given to the study of the process of transforming knowledge from a variety of sources into a body of professional knowledge for teaching, we are beginning to see the complexity of preparing individuals to teach. Simply telling someone that they should behave in certain ways or use specific strategies will not accomplish the task. Nor will clinical experience alone do the job. The task of educating teachers is one of facilitating cognitive transformations that can be assessed through observations of practice and reflections on that practice. Learning to transform knowledge into practice is the heart of the enterprise.

CONSIDERATION TWO: LAYING THE GROUNDWORK FOR TEACHER LEARNING

The knowledge base for teaching is accumulated over many years from many sources: research findings, disciplinary study, classroom experience, work with students, observation of expert teachers, reflections on one's own practice, and conversations with thoughtful practitioners. Teacher education programs, on the other hand, are typically of extremely short duration. Many secondary programs, for example, comprise no more than three or four courses, sometimes accompanied by limited field experience and followed by a student teaching experience. Since it is impossible during an initial preparation program to study deeply—or even to introduce—all of the knowledge that teachers might use as they carry out their work, decisions must be made by program faculty about what is most critical for beginning teachers to know. Teacher educators, thus, must exercise great selectivity about the knowledge claims presented by advocates of different conceptions of the teacher's work. This is a difficult task for two reasons. There is a lack of consensus among the communities of teachers and teacher educators about essential knowledge. As stated earlier, the fact that different scholars have advocated different priorities for beginning teachers and different views of what constitutes adequate knowledge complicates this task. Furthermore, there is a tendency for those who educate teachers either to want to produce a "complete" teacher at the end of a program or to assume that learning to teach is solely a matter of experience. Thus, programs of teacher education differ widely in the level of knowledge and expertise that is expected of program graduates. If we accept that knowledge is cumulative, then we must be willing to engage in some tough conceptualizing about what knowledge is essential, and then set some specific limits on what is included in initial programs of teacher preparation. We must also recognize that learning to teach is a career-long endeavor that needs to be thoughtfully conceived as developing over time as a result of inquiry, experience, and reflection.

CONSIDERATION THREE: PROGRAMMATIC DECISIONS ON WHAT KNOWLEDGE IS TAUGHT

The content selected for inclusion in programs of teacher education must be carefully conceived and relevant for beginning teachers, and it must be capable of being taught within the context of program constraints. Questions of program purposes, as well as availability of resources, play important roles in these decisions. For example, if a program's purpose is to train novices to use specific teaching or management techniques, these purposes can be achieved through a variety of training methods. Practice in using and refining the skill will be more effective, however, if the training occurs in real classrooms with real learners. Understanding when and with whom to use these skills will be further enhanced if contextual factors are also taken into account. The implications become apparent when program purposes go beyond learning that a particular skill or disposition is essential for pupil learning to learning how to use the skill in an actual teaching situation. The approach that goes beyond providing opportunities for prospective teachers to learn about the skill and why it should be developed is more costly than simply talking about these matters; it also includes providing opportunities to observe expert teachers using the skill, to discuss with them conditions that support its effectiveness and ones that do not, and to practice—with guidance, support, and reflection—the development of the skill. Extending the study of teaching into actual teaching situations goes far beyond assigning students to work in classrooms. It requires that purposes of classroom experience be thoughtfully contrived and carefully orchestrated and evaluated to include mentoring by expert teachers and teacher educators.

The principle is the same with regard to other worthwhile content. If, for example, a program's purpose is to develop in novices the propensities for fostering a learning community environment within the classroom, connections must be built between theoretical frameworks that undergird the concept of learning community and the learners who are its participants. Prospective teachers must themselves participate in learning communities so that they can construct meanings from first-hand experiences. These experiences must include opportunities to participate as members of several communities and must help create a community within the everyday realities of the classroom and the school. Thus, the intention to prepare teachers who will foster personal and social responsibility among their students implies that teacher education students will have opportunities to come to understand the concepts and principles embedded in relevant theory. Such purposes also require that teacher education students have opportunities to study practice with these theories in mind, to attempt various approaches to accomplishing the purposes, and to reflect on outcomes with experienced teachers and teacher educators.

At issue here is the fundamental question of how novices can most effectively come to understand and be able to demonstrate through their practice that they have developed a knowledge base that is sufficient for beginning to teach in a professional manner. Depending on a program's purposes, different priorities will be established for what content is included in the program. Further, if the purposes identified indicate the need for special resources (such as regular and continuing access to a classroom of students, knowledgeable faculty who can provide the particular content that has been identified, and a financial base that supports the collaborative work in schools), then the question of available resources becomes critical. In some cases, programmatic decisions may need to be made that limit the knowledge that can be presented and experienced. And, at times, some goals may be modified in light of scarce resources. It is essential that such decisions are consistent with the best available scholarship and are grounded in a thoughtful conception of professional teaching.

CONSIDERATION FOUR: THE IMPORTANCE OF FRAMING THE KNOWLEDGE

Programmatic decisions influence more than just what knowledge is presented in a particular program of teacher education. Whatever programmatic content is selected and included in a specific teacher education program must be framed in a way that supports student learning. As Valli & Tom (1988) point out, the same content can be framed in different ways. Since the framework within which the content is embedded will influence both what novices pay attention to and how they make sense of the information, Valli & Tom suggest that the way the content is organized, presented, and justified may be as important as the content itself. For some faculty, framing the content of the curriculum in different ways will be quite challenging and will require that they become learners themselves.

For faculty to learn how to do this framing, it is essential that they become inquirers into their own teaching practices and study seriously what contributes to their students' learning. Since this distinction is centrally concerned with understanding the nature of the learner in teacher education, namely, preservice students, teacher educators must become inquirers about all aspects of their students' learning.

Understanding the processes through which novices acquire the knowledge, skills, and propensities they need is also a critical part of the knowledge base for a teacher education program. Developing the teacher candidate's capacity to study, analyze, and provide exemplary practice entails exposing prospective teachers to alternative frames for what to look for in teaching situations. It also involves thoughtful consideration of standards for appraising what is seen and done. While it is true that novices must acquire the knowledge about subject matter, students, learning, contexts, teaching, and schools that can inform their professional judgments and actions, they must also experience making judgments and taking action. Initially, this may be done by analyzing cases and working within limited teaching situations, but later, it must occur within the context of consequential classroom practice.

Further, an important but often overlooked factor in making decisions about how to frame knowledge in teacher education is the prior knowledge of the teacher candidates. Potential teachers often believe they already know how to teach, and many see their certification program as troublesome and unnecessary. Despite the obvious flaws in their understandings about teaching, these views are not easily changed (Ball, 1988; Ball & McDiarmid, 1988; Grossman, 1990; Wilson & Wineburg, 1988). More important for program faculty, however, is the fact that these perspectives, if unchallenged and unaltered, typically inhibit the development of the professional knowledge base desired. This point was illustrated in a recent study of juniors in a language arts methods course (Florio-Ruane & Lensmire, 1990). Although resisted by students, who found the experience painful, confronting novices with knowledge about children and their writing that contradicted their well-established perceptions of what these learners could do, led to a gradual transformation in their conceptions about teaching writing in schools. Consequently, faculty must come to some fundamental agreements about their conceptions of how novices learn to teach, if they are to frame an adequate knowledge base for their teacher education program.

CONSIDERATION FIVE: FACTORS INVOLVED IN BUILDING A KNOWLEDGE BASE

The question of how novices build a knowledge base must be seriously considered and provides the basis for both what is taught and how the program is organized and enacted. Two examples illustrate this point. The first has to do with the importance of structuring a program to provide for group membership and socialization. The second deals with the importance of relating theoretical and practical knowledge during initial instruction.

As part of Whitworth College's Exxon project, a study was conducted of differences in the knowledge bases of expert and novice teachers (Michaelis, 1989). The study focused on the knowledge, beliefs, meanings, and contexts within which expert teachers teach. The study also examined the thinking and perspectives behind the actions of exceptional teachers and the origin of those understandings. The purpose was to uncover personal meanings behind the methods used by these outstanding teachers. Three domains of influence emerged from the data as having shaped the teaching frames of the teachers studied: the teachers' personal history, their affiliations, and the context of their current teaching assignments. These influences appeared to interact to form the teachers' frames of reference for what a good teacher does and is.

The significance of membership, both personal and professional, in the development of the teachers' frames of reference for teaching was particularly salient. Membership for the purpose of the study was any voluntary affiliation with a certain group or association, including not only formal groups, but any collective, formal or informal, large or small, defined or undefined, with which the teachers expressed strong affiliation. Such memberships were important to the teachers in helping them bring meaning to their work and define their beliefs and tasks. Because members of a culture share common purposes and norms, or frames of reference, membership in a group provided a shared orientation for these teachers. This phenomenon highlights the importance of providing for such group affiliation as part of the structure of a preservice program and helps to explain the success of programs that have organized their programs around cohorts of students and faculty. Interestingly, teachers in the Whitworth study who reported few or no significant memberships outside of their immediate teaching context appeared to have frames of reference that were shaped primarily by conforming to their early teaching experiences and tended to be more traditional in character. Such findings suggest that enculturation is one way to create a foundation for knowledge growth among beginning teachers. When those enculturation experiences are consistent with the goals of the program, they can add an important dimension to the learning experience.

The first phase of the Michigan State University Exxon project also investigated differences in the knowledge bases of experienced and novice teachers, with a particular emphasis on identifying knowledge that is critical for beginning teachers. This study engaged teachers and authors of six of the chapters from the KBBT volume in a discussion of the relevance of the authors' conceptions of critical knowledge to the demands of teaching experienced by these teachers. Teachers in this study supported the views of critical knowledge domains presented in the volume, but discussions about how teachers used such knowledge revealed that experienced teachers no longer saw these domains as distinct from one another. Discussions about discrete domains of knowledge seemed artificial and were difficult. Inevitably, the discussions turned to ways that decisions primarily concerning one domain were influenced by knowledge stemming from another domain. This was particularly true during discussions concerning the chapters on subject matter knowledge and subject-specific pedagogy. The teachers' knowledge was clearly organized into networks of understanding and was best described as being contextualized.

This characterization is consistent with the findings of other investigations of expert-novice differences in knowledge systems that are readily accessible during interactive teaching. For example, Borko and Livingston (1989) describe differences between experts and novices in planning, improvisational teaching, and post-lesson reflection. They suggest that novices be helped to develop knowledge structures that integrate knowledge of content and how to represent it with knowledge of students and the contexts of the teaching situation. As Florio-Ruane (1989) points out, however, one could argue that novices also "contextualize" knowledge about teaching and learning due to their apprenticeship of observation. This observation suggests that teacher education programs should provide opportunities for students to engage in conscious examinations and evaluations of the background knowledge they bring into such situations and help them to reconceptualize the relationships among these factors.

These insights also support the notion that prospective teachers should study teaching and learning in actual classrooms so that they can tie their examined conceptions of teaching and learning to the realities of teaching and learning in different contexts. Furthermore, these findings provide compelling evidence for a constructivist view of teacher education. Such a view recognizes that individual teachers must construct their own frameworks for teaching. The kinds of knowledge needed must be acquired from focused experience in schools as well as from disciplined study at a university. Yet unexamined, experience is not necessarily educative (Feiman-Nemser & Buchmann, 1986). Thus, any reform of teacher education must involve the design of a program structure that integrates theoretical and practical knowledge by weaving together knowledge drawn from both of these sources into a coherent, comprehensive conceptual framework.

CONSIDERATION SIX: JUSTIFYING THE KNOWLEDGE BASE

The conceptual framework for a teacher education program must be capable of withstanding scrutiny from the scholarly communities of both university and school practitioners. Not only must teacher educators deem the content to be important, but practicing teachers must recognize the importance of the curriculum in their daily professional lives. Thus, the content that is included must be relevant, adequate, and it must be seen as essential for beginning teachers by those who prepare them, those who hire them, and those who work with them.

Criteria for judging the adequacy and appropriateness of the teacher education curriculum need to be developed and used to bring some sharper focus to the enterprise. Such criteria should encompass both design and delivery aspects of the curriculum. These criteria should foster the development of programs that will be both relevant for preparing wise practitioners for today's schools and sensitive to new professional roles and images that might be created by teaching professionals in the next century. Developing such criteria will require the collaborative work of educators who can envision such new roles and who further understand the multifaceted nature of teacher knowledge and the influences on the development of a knowledge base for teacher education.

The implications of the need to justify the content of a teacher education program are significant. Teacher educators must be able to articulate the purposes and rationale of their programs and to demonstrate how the program design and delivery are presumed to accomplish these aims. The need for justifying a curriculum also calls into question the prevalent practice of conveying theoretical perspectives on teaching in isolation from the experience of teaching. This practice stems from the implicit belief that knowledge can be decontextualized and understood apart from the context in which it is used. This belief is now being questioned and alternative propositions are being explored (Brown, Collins, & Duguid, 1989) that suggest that this assumption inevitably limits the effectiveness of such practices.

CONCLUSION

Given these six considerations, the role of the knowledge base for teaching in the redesign of teacher education might be represented in a program description that clearly articulates the conception of teaching and learning that the program is advancing. The statement should explicate the professional roles, responsibilities, dispositions, capacities, and related practices that graduates are expected to exemplify upon completing the program. It should describe the nature of required coursework and educational experiences and should explicate standards for monitoring and evaluating students' progress. Furthermore, the statement should present a conceptual framework that clarifies the sources of knowledge included in the program and that demonstrates how that knowledge is presumed to influence professional judgment and practice. The processes through which students are expected to accommodate program content should be integral to the knowledge base of the program and should be clearly justified in scholarly terms. Finally, criteria for judging program quality should specify objective evidence that can be examined by other members of the scholarly community.

Described in this way, efforts to redesign teacher education intertwine thoughtful conceptions of teaching with concerns for how novices will develop the intellectual, dispositional, and performance capacities embodied within the images of teaching that guide the redesign work. Without such deliberate planning, the temptation to confuse means and ends is everpresent. Just as teacher educators urge classroom teachers to select activities and strategies purposefully, teacher education faculty must also be willing to lay out their intentions and select those approaches that, in their view, hold the greatest promise for achieving the ends they have specified. The importance of being self-critical and of evaluating program outcomes quickly becomes apparent when faculties attempt to reconceptualize their work.

As a field, we are just beginning to study how teachers learn to teach and what formal teacher education programs contribute to that process (National Center for Research on Teacher Education, 1988). Our task is made more difficult by the lack of good information about productive ways to proceed. Furthermore, there are few examples of effective, innovative ways to accomplish our goals for initial teacher education. While the need to consider the structure of the program within which essential content is embedded is now recognized (Howey & Zimpher, 1989), changes in the structure of teacher education programs are still few and slow to reach fruition. Often viewed by critics as an indication of teacher educators' unwillingness or inability to reform themselves, this circumstance exists despite ongoing institutional efforts to reform programs (The Holmes Group, 1988). On the contrary, the slowness with which promising reform is realized is more a reflection of the extraordinarily difficult conceptual and practical concerns that must be addressed within the process of change itself. These issues represent some of the major challenges in transforming knowledge about teaching into programs of teacher education, and it is these challenges that will be addressed in Section Two of this volume.

■

REFERENCES

Ball, D., & McDiarmid, W. (1988). Research on teacher learning: Studying how teachers' knowledge changes. *Action in Teacher Education, 10*(2), 17-24.

Ball, D. L. (1988). *Knowledge and reasoning in mathematical pedagogy: Examining what prospective teachers bring to teacher education.* Unpublished doctoral dissertation, Michigan State University, East Lansing.

Barnes, H. (1989). Structuring knowledge for beginning teaching. In M. C. Reynolds (Ed.), *Knowledge base for the beginning teacher* (pp. 13-22). Oxford, England: Pergamon.

Brown, J. S., Collins, A., & Duguid, P. (1989). Situated cognition and the culture of learning. *Educational Researcher, 18*(1), 32-42.

Borko, H., & Livingston, C. (1989). Cognition and improvisation differences in mathematics instruction by expert and novice teachers. *American Educational Research Journal, 26*(4), 473-495.

Connelly, F. M., & Clandinin, D. J. (1986). On narrative method, personal philosophy, and narrative unities in the story of teaching. *Journal of Research in Science Teaching, 23*(4), 283-310.

Cross, K. P. (1990, October). *Teachers as scholars.* Paper presented at the national conference on "The New American Scholar: The Scholarship of Teaching," Iona College, New Rochelle, NY.

Elbaz, F. (1987). Teachers' knowledge of teaching: Strategies for reflection. In J. Smyth (Ed.), *Educating Teachers: Changing the Nature of Pedagogical Knowledge* (pp. 45-53). London: Falmer.

Feiman-Nemser, S., & Buchmann, M. (1986). *Knowing, thinking, and doing in learning to teach: A research framework and some initial results* (Research Series No. 180). East Lansing: Michigan State University, Institute for Research on Teaching.

Florio-Ruane, S. (1989). Social organization of classes and schools. In M.C. Reynolds (Ed.), *Knowledge base for the beginning teacher* (pp. 163-172). Oxford, England: Pergamon.

Florio-Ruane, S., & Lensmire, T. (1990). Transforming future teachers' ideas about writing instruction. *Journal of Curriculum Studies, 22*, 277-289.

■

Grossman, P. L. (1990). Subject matter knowledge and the teaching of English. In J. Brophy (Ed.), *Advances in research on teaching* (Vol. 2). Greenwich, CT: JAI Press.

The Holmes Group. (1988). *Work in Progress: The Holmes Group One Year On.* East Lansing, MI: Author.

Howey, K. R., & Zimpher, N. L. (1989). *Profiles of preservice teacher education: Inquiry into the nature of programs.* Albany: State University of New York Press.

Kennedy, M. (1987). *Inexact sciences: Teacher education and learning to teach* (Issue Paper 87-2). East Lansing: Michigan State University, National Center for Research on Teacher Education.

Lampert, M., & Clark, C. M. (1990). Expert knowledge and expert thinking in teaching: A response to Floden and Klinzing. *Educational Researcher, 19*(4), 21-23.

Michaelis, R. (1989). *Study of expert elementary teachers.* Unpublished manuscript, Whitworth College, Spokane, WA.

National Center for Research on Teacher Education. (1988). *Dialogues in teacher education.* (Issue Paper 88-4). East Lansing: Michigan State University, National Center for Research on Teacher Education.

Shulman, L. (1987). Knowledge and teaching: Foundations of the new reform. *Harvard Educational Review, 57,* 1-22.

Tom, A. R., & Valli, L. (1990). Professional knowledge for teachers. In W. Houston (Ed.), *Handbook of research on teacher education* (pp. 373-390). New York: Macmillan.

Valli, L., & Tom, A. R. (1988). How adequate are the knowledge base frameworks in teacher education? *Journal of Teacher Education, 39*(5), 5-12.

Wilson, S., & Wineburg, S. (1988). Peering at history through different lenses: The role of disciplinary perspectives in teaching history. *Teachers College Record, 89*(4), 525-539.

Zeichner, K. (1981). Alternative paradigms of teacher education. *Journal of Teacher Education, 34*(3), 3-9.

THE KBBT AND THE PREPARATION OF TEACHERS FOR CONTEMPORARY AMERICAN SOCIETY: AN UNMATCHED SET?

2

MARLEEN C. PUGACH

BRENDA H. LEAKE

Overview. Without question, the pluralistic nature of the society in which we live creates a set of challenges for the preparation of teachers that is unlike any for which teachers have previously been prepared. In this regard, the specific questions raised in this chapter are: How does the framing of this volume, which purports to represent the knowledge base for the preparation of all novice teachers, contribute to educating teachers for contemporary American society, a society that is fundamentally characterized by a multiethnic, multiracial population? Is the point of view presented across the chapters in the KBBT volume unified in this regard? Should it be? What is the responsibility of those whose work is thought to represent the most current knowledge for presenting their findings in the context of the society in which it will be used? Or, is it largely the responsibility of its consumers—in this case, teacher educators—to draw the explicit connections between what is considered to represent the best current scholarly knowledge regarding teaching (in contrast to knowledge regarding teacher education) and its social context? ■

While a great deal of controversy continues to exist regarding the concept of a knowledge base for teaching, its emergence as a metaphor for the professionalization of teaching has signaled a period of critical reflection for those who are engaged in the preparation of teachers. That codifiable knowledge for teaching exists for informing, as opposed to prescribing the work of teachers, and that this knowledge compels teachers to make reflective judgments regarding its use, seems to us a reasonable state of affairs. Research on teaching and learning holds the potential both to strengthen teachers' practical arguments (Fenstermacher, 1986), and to decrease teachers' uncertainties (Floden & Klinzing, 1990). However, how such knowledge is codified and presented to encourage its optimal use by those who design programs of teacher education represents another dimension of the issue. Tom and Valli (1990) remind us that the context in which knowledge is presented centrally affects how such knowledge is conceptualized by its users.

The purpose of this chapter is to place the initial effort, as represented by the KBBT volume, in the context of the society in which teachers will go about their work. Specifically, our concern lies with the relationship between the knowledge base as it is presented in the KBBT volume, and the particular society for whose children teachers are being prepared today.

We have organized our critique of the knowledge base volume into four sections. First, we discuss the actual and implied portrayal of minority students in the various chapters of the volume. Second, we discuss areas in which the knowledge, as presented, holds important implications for the education of a diverse student population, but where those implications have been omitted or glossed over in a way that disallows an explicit linkage between that portion of the knowledge base and the education of a multiracial, multiethnic population of students. Third, we examine the degree to which the volume addresses issues of the relationship between family and the schools, including collaboration between parents and teachers. Finally, we propose an alternative view for conceptualizing the knowledge base, one which integrates knowledge and the particular context and human dimensions unique to teaching. This alternative would more fully validate the notion that the education process is nested in, and must be responsive to, a richly diverse cultural milieu of the America of the 1990s and beyond.

THE KBBT VOLUME'S PORTRAYAL OF MINORITY STUDENTS

Four chapters (Cazden and Mehan, Florio-Ruane, Greene, and Reynolds) appear to deal directly with issues related to the nature of contemporary society, and the relationship between teacher education and that society. Cazden and Mehan (1989) recognize from the outset that the "unprecedented nature of teacher-student relationships" results from the singular fact that, more so than ever before, "teachers and students will not share cultural and social experiences" (Cazden & Mehan, 1989, p. 47). This simple statement guides their subsequent discussions of task context, classroom language and culture, grouping practices, and home and community relationships. Their perspective includes the critical notions for teachers that: (1) intelligence is not monolithic and absolute, but rather situation-specific; (2) accommodating children's cultural backgrounds is one of the basic responsibilities of teachers; (3) prosocial grouping practices are important alternatives to conventional tracking, which historically penalizes minority and poor students; and (4) understanding and accommodating students' cultures are essential for success when teachers and students do not share a common culture.

Cazden and Mehan's chapter presents a comprehensive view of some of the major difficulties facing teacher education, if it is to keep pace with the nature of contemporary American society. They challenge the practice of "blaming the victim," and rightfully portray "the need for beginning teachers to vary instructional circumstances in order to take full advantage of students' often unrecognized resources" (p. 49). Cazden and Mehan clearly value the cultural capital which minority students bring to their own and other students' educational setting, and provide consistent direction for overcoming the deficit model that has often been wrongly embraced in education.

Florio-Ruane (1989) focuses her discourse primarily around the importance of beginning teachers possessing a thorough understanding of the communicative processes in schools. She discusses the potential difficulties faced by beginning teachers as they attempt to make professional sense of the already familiar environment of the classroom. Inherent in the process of ferreting out professional norms, beginning teachers must become fluent in the knowledge, skills, beliefs, values, and languages of the cultural context of the schools in which they teach. Additionally, Florio-Ruane speaks directly to the potentially negative impact that the school's cultural norms might have on students who come to classroom settings from backgrounds inconsistent with the prevalent school culture.

While Florio-Ruane's chapter is far more culturally enlightened and responsible than many of the other writings set forth in the KBBT volume, she weakens her position with a subsection entitled "The Special Problems of Minority Children." Although the basic content of this portion of her chapter emphasizes the notion that culturally diverse students are not inherently deficient, but that the deficiencies lie within educators who have been inadequately or inappropriately trained to work in the realities of the culturally pluralistic American schools, the prejudicial wording of the subtitle implies the old, too familiar, mindset of "blaming the victim." Admittedly, in isolation, the selection of a subtitle may seem to be a petty issue. However, in the context of the KBBT volume's patterns of omissions and deleterious commentary with respect to culturally diverse students, the selection of a subtitle becomes an issue of far greater significance.

Differing from both the Cazden and Mehan chapter and the Florio-Ruane chapter, Reynolds' contribution on special needs students (Reynolds, 1989) ascribes a completely different context for thinking about what it means to be a member of a racial or ethnic minority. In addition to students who are behind academically, who have poor social behavior, or physical or health limitations, Reynolds defines students with special needs as any child who lives in poverty, whose primary language is other than English, or who has limited "experiences which provide background for formal education" (Reynolds, 1989, p. 130). By using the term "special needs" to describe this broad segment of the population, Reynolds promotes a conceptualization of all students who live in poverty or who are bilingual as deficient, thus discounting the potential of their culturally different background experiences in their education. This unfortunate, inclusive definition of special needs students is followed by a conventional discussion of the history of services to students labeled as handicapped. Later in the chapter Reynolds goes on to include in his definition children of divorced parents, children living with single mothers, children of alcoholic parents, and children of teenage mothers all under the rubric of students with special needs.

The approach to the multiethnic, multiracial, and multiclass society in which we live appears in this chapter to be squarely based in a deficit model. The discussion is predicated on the assumption that all students who live in poverty, who are bilingual, as well as those who are disabled, require special education services.

Rather than promoting the viewpoint that the student population has changed, and that this change requires drastic rethinking of our educational approaches to all children, Reynolds (1989) labels a huge segment of the population of children in our schools as special needs (SN), stating that "the main work of educators who serve SN pupils is to join with other educators in efforts to make sure that the well-confirmed principles of effective instruction and effective schools are applied in programs for SN pupils" (p. 135). His assumption, in this statement, appears to be that the broad group of children he identified earlier will all have special teachers, and, by extension, that not all teachers will teach students who fall into one of the many categories he names as belonging to special needs. This is obviously not the case.

Reynolds makes some important comments with respect to generalized knowledge for all teachers. However, these attempts are dwarfed in relationship to the decidedly deficit-oriented nature of the chapter; further, his position is often inconsistent. For example, in discussing the importance of teachers understanding families that are culturally and ethnically different, Reynolds cites the importance of seeing a child's cultural background as a contribution to his education. Yet he talks about identifying SN students on the basis of a lack of background preparation. He calls for ending school programs that regularly result in poor achievement for urban children and youth, and the need for teachers to be willing to be inclusive of all students in their classes. Yet he states that teachers of special needs students should insure the quality of programs for SN pupils alone.

In intent, the chapter seems to reflect confusion; is its purpose to provide a contemporary view of special education, one that includes more than the small number of students with actual handicapping conditions? Or is it to discuss the changes in the school-aged population, changes that will demand a new way of dealing equitably with the whole school population, without calling many special needs and others not? Given the actual rhetoric of the chapter, neither of these seems to be the prominent message, although both ideas are mentioned in passing. What dominates is the stark portrayal of the vast majority of students in today's schools as having special needs presented in the context of the special education sector of the educational bureaucracy. That students have many extraordinary needs in our schools today is not at issue here. What is at issue is the unfortunate misrepresentation of the task ahead for teachers and teacher educators, as it pertains to their expectations for working with children who are culturally and ethnically different, children raised in poverty, and children with handicapping conditions.

In bold contrast, Greene (1989) uses her chapter as an opportunity to establish a firm rationale for teacher preparation programs to encompass three major challenges of contemporary American education: (1) American schools must expand the charge of democratic socialization to include preparation of an "articulate public," a reflective citizenry; (2) teachers must be knowledgeable about the overt and covert ways in which schools are affected by the interrelated social and political contexts in which they exist; and (3) the racial, ethnic, and socioeconomic diversity of American society necessitates schooling which recognizes, and even celebrates, the pluralistic capital of contemporary America. Greene emphasizes the importance of preparing beginning teachers who are themselves empowered by and who can, in turn, empower their students with the knowledge that schools exist within interrelated social and political contexts—contents which define educational goals—and the distribution of educational benefits in a manner consistent with prevailing societal beliefs and values. Subsequently, she challenges those who wish to become educators of American youth to be cognizant of, and responsive to, the increasingly diverse American population and the resultant changes in societal and political educational expectations. The pluralistic composition of contemporary America necessitates that educators become aware of the influences of the "multiple realities and multiple perspectives" (Greene, 1989, p. 144) which affect the social and political contexts of schools.

Beginning with the 19th century and continuing through to the current era of high technology, Greene presents a concise, yet effective, overview of the major shifts in the American social and political arena which have had significant impact on our educational system. She openly acknowledges the embarrassing legacy of the racial, ethnic, socioeconomic, and sexual exclusivity which has too often been prevalent in the American educational agenda. Greene cites Tyack and Hansot in reminding us that the charge to American schools has historically been "to preserve—but improve—the existing social order" (1989, p. 146). This charge has usually implicitly, and often explicitly, meant that the status and values of white, middle-class, Protestant males must be maintained as the standard by which all others are measured. Greene quotes E.L. Doctorow in describing the relative contextual stature of African American and other minorities, "There were no Negroes. There were no immigrants" (p. 146). The educational context has traditionally rendered African Americans and other minorities to relative invisibility. Greene states that prior to the early 1960s, racist attitudes relegated African Americans to positions of either intentional exclusion, or invisible menial existence.

Ironically, as Greene so eloquently establishes this historical context for the beginning teacher's knowledge base, she exposes what we perceive to be the critical problem of the KBBT volume in its present form. If contemporary American schools exist in, and are held accountable to, a highly pluralistic society, it appears inadequate and inaccurate to present a presumably definitive body of writings which only infrequently make direct references to African Americans and other American minority youth. Discussions of culturally diverse populations are primarily either the presentation of deficit perspectives, or completely absent. Thus, the KBBT volume relegates African Americans and other American minorities to menial status or nonexistence. By the omission of, or negativity toward, the ever-growing culturally diverse American population, the KBBT volume reflects the unfortunate realities of those attitudes commonly found in both the schools and teacher education programs. We do not believe that a work which purports to lend a conceptual framework for teacher education in the 1990s should leave to chance the critical social and political translations which must be made by American educators in a culturally diverse context.

■

EXPLICIT LINKS BETWEEN THE KBBT VOLUME AND TEACHERS FOR CONTEMPORARY CLASSROOMS

The issue we attempt to address in this section of our critique is the degree to which implications for teaching in a multiethnic, multiracial society need to be drawn explicitly in the presentation of current knowledge for teaching. Our concern is that there are many aspects of the recent research on learning and learners that have profound implications for how teachers approach their work with a diverse group of students. However, if those implications are not

■ ■

explicitly drawn, teacher educators and their students may fail to connect the meaning of that knowledge to the nature of the students they teach. If knowledge is presented in the abstract, in the absence of these linkages, the danger exists that beginning teachers will fail to see its relevance to their own teaching of students whose culture and race differs from their own, particularly when novice teachers may not yet have explored their own feelings regarding working in multiracial, multiethnic schools or classrooms. For teacher educators themselves, similar potential exists for incomplete or incorrect interpretations.

The critical need to make these links in an explicit manner was apparently obvious to Griffin (1989) as expressed in the final chapter of the volume. Griffin does a commendable job of summarizing the major theoretical components of the KBBT volume into 10 "overlapping and interactive" theoretical premises. He terms these theoretical premises as "features," and discusses each one in the context of a functional, contemporary, educational environment. The "Features of the Knowledge-Based School" presented by Griffin are: (1) knowledge about teaching is mutable and always under consideration for modification; (2) teaching is complex, often ambiguous, and frequently nonlinear; (3) learning to teach is additive, ongoing, and unending; (4) teaching and schooling are examined in light of current and historical context conditions; (5) both pedagogical knowledge and subject matter knowledge are valued; (6) knowledge is actively constructed by students, with considerable participation by teachers; (7) teachers are curriculum workers; (8) curriculum and instruction are coherent and systematic over time, and across grades and subjects; (9) theories, research, and practical wisdom influence school programs, pedagogy, and the ways the school accomplishes its tasks; and (10) teachers demonstrate the hallmarks of professional behavior. Following the more abstract discourse on these premises, Griffin makes a transition into a more concrete venue by offering illustrative, hypothetical vignettes as "glimpses of life in the knowledge-driven school" (Griffin, 1989, p. 284).

In presenting and discussing each of these premises and vignettes, Griffin (1989) makes salient connections between the body of knowledge offered in the KBBT volume and the issues and realities of contemporary American schools. Griffin charges those professionals engaged in teacher education to develop a collective sense of purpose, similar to that imperative for the professionalization of classroom practitioners, which is clearly reflective of an ecological perspective of the teaching/learning process. He states that "if this book becomes a useful resource for teacher educators, it will be necessary for each of us to give some conscious attention to how the various bodies of knowledge important to teachers can come together in reinforcing and intellectually and practically rigorous ways" (p. 283).

Unfortunately, the KBBT volume has relegated one of the most useful chapters to the "last-but-not-least" status. Because the chapters can be read in isolation, the absence of any ongoing framework for linking the knowledge beyond Griffin's final chapter to contemporary American schools and school-aged children and youth is particularly problematic. A few examples, illustrating what might occur without such an organizing framework, follow.

A thorough knowledge of research on the cognitive-mediational perspective on learning is fundamental to the repertoire of a beginning teacher precisely because, as Anderson states (1989), of the advantage this perspective provides in the sense that "it is less likely to lead to beliefs that students cannot learn" (Anderson, 1989, p. 105). Anderson stresses that instruction cannot take place without knowledge of the learner and his or her existing knowledge. However, Anderson fails to use this chapter as an opportunity to provide specific examples which clarify that we are often talking about students from other cultures and ethnic groups whose background knowledge is not lacking, but instead is merely different from the culture of most teachers and needs to be appreciated and made familiar as such. In other words, teachers for contemporary American schools will necessarily have to expect these vast differences. And even if they do not teach students whose culture differs vastly from their own, which we believe is unlikely for any teacher, they are still responsible for transmitting values which are inclusive of heterogeneity. Jackson's (1986) notion of the mistaken "presumption of shared identity" is precisely the lesson of the cognitive-mediational perspective; promoting the expectation for children's differences in background knowledge, and teaching how to be appreciative of these differences are basic considerations for all programs of teacher preparation. The lack of explicit linkages between the fundamental concept of mediating learning from the point at which students enter the classroom and the knowledge they bring to the learning process—and the immediate problem in contemporary American schools of the endemic failures of students whose background knowledge is not that of middle-class America—is perhaps the most critical example of this concept.

Further, without specific examples and linkages, discussions of the importance of background knowledge may unwittingly reinforce negative stereotypes. For example, when Anderson states in Chapter Nine that the

teacher's presentation of materials is crucial for "students who do not sponta-
neously search for meaningful relationships between ideas (i.e., younger students,
lower-achieving students, special needs students, or students who are novices in a
particular domain)" (Anderson, 1989, p. 102), there is a real danger that this could
be interpreted as "students in inner city schools, children of poverty, do not search
for meaningful relationships between ideas" and, thus, be incorrectly generalized to
entire urban or rural poor populations. Great care needs to be taken in the presentation of research-based knowledge (Tom & Valli, 1990) to insure that its interpretation extends and challenges conventional experiences prospective teachers
may have had. In the abstract, without contextualizing that knowledge in terms of
contemporary American society, the aims of teacher education relative to the
purpose of democracy are not likely to be fostered.

A related problem presents itself in Wang and Palincsar's
(1989) chapter on students' active roles in learning. In general, the chapter is predicated on the important concept that

> an understanding of students' knowledge characteristics is essential for the design
> and improvement of instructional interventions, especially interventions directed
> toward the proportionally large population of students who have not benefited from
> the outcomes-focused approach that dominates current practice. (Wang & Palincsar,
> 1989, p. 74)

However, it is possible that the abstract presentation of
this idea may not stimulate a connection between the experiences of many minority
students in schools and those concepts. For example, in a discussion of the importance of perceptions of self and learning, the role of self-perceptions regarding
past experience is stressed as it relates to effects on a student's subsequent
performance. To discuss this aspect of teaching and learning without making a
linkage to the vast numbers of students who come to school with negative experiences behind them is at best incomplete. In contrast, McDiarmid, Ball, and
Anderson (1989) provide a specific and extremely helpful example of how the
concept of equality may be understood differently in the Yupik Eskimo culture
to illustrate the role of culture in the construction of knowledge and the importance of simultaneously considering subject matter and the students for whom
it is being addressed.

The inherent problem in omitting these connections in
the KBBT volume involves the degree to which those who would codify the current
knowledge base see its compilation either as an abstract, or a contextualized task.

In our opinion, the current state of schooling requires attention to context as teachers draw on the knowledge base; without it, we simply may miss a perfect opportunity to make explicit how current basic concepts of teaching and learning play out in a demographically heterogeneous society. The decreasing efficacy of far too many public schools is salient evidence of the "academic bankruptcy" which occurs when practice ignores contextual realities. We worry about the implications of its omission for developing responsive schools. Helping prospective teachers overcome their stereotypes is hard work, and it is questionable to assume that novices will make the connections that will help them overcome their stereotypes easily.

■

SCHOOLS, FAMILIES, AND COMMUNITIES AND THE KBBT VOLUME

A third area of concern relates to knowledge about how the school and families/communities interact. Largely unacknowledged in the interpretation of the knowledge base advanced in the KBBT volume is knowledge related to working with parents and families of school-age children. The notion of home-school relations, so prevalent in the literature and practice of early childhood education, is generally conspicuous by its absence. "Parent-teacher cooperation" is listed on one page in the volume's subject index. Similarly, "community influence" is listed on two pages (one of which is the same page as the parental reference); both of these references are located in Griffin's final chapter. A single reference to communities and school districts occurs in the chapter of the organization and governance of school districts. In other words, nowhere is the critical issue of building partnerships with parents addressed in the context of specific knowledge for teaching. Further, the whole notion of early childhood education and prevention is also excluded from the volume. Unfortunately, the chapter on collaboration, which provides a likely opportunity to include collaboration among teachers as well as between teachers and parents, was not so conceptualized. Parents are mentioned primarily in the context of special education in this chapter as well as in Reynolds' chapter.

■　■

Contemporary American schools are perhaps most unlike those in the past regarding the degree of voluntary parental involvement in the education of children and youth. For a variety of reasons, parents have become increasingly distanced from the formal education of their children. While the most commonly accepted rationales for this distancing tend to be related to socioeconomic factors, there are those who might argue that the diminishing parental investments in schools are the result of increased parental awareness of educational quality, or lack thereof. Nationally, schools are addressing items such as decentralization of school bureaucracies, school voucher plans, and school choice plans; the very nature of these issues indicate a more proactive posturing of parents as more informed and critical consumers of education. These issues of increased quantity and quality of parental access to the educational arena, coupled with the literature certifying the importance of familial connections in the learning of all students, necessitate an intensive level of consideration when compiling and prioritizing a knowledge base for beginning teachers. Perhaps the KBBT volume's minimal recognition of crucial issues around family connections is indicative of the isolationist attitudes prevalent in most schools relative to parental participation and access. How teachers address this, how they understand different familial structures, how they make the jump from "parental" involvement to "family" involvement—thereby recognizing that other family members may also be in a position to link to schools, and how to build extended parental and family support are simply not addressed. In short, we find this to be a major shortcoming of the volume, one which cannot be omitted if schools are to be responsive to their student populations.

THE UNIQUENESS OF THE KNOWLEDGE BASE FOR TEACHING

In the press to present teaching as a wholly scientific endeavor, those who would codify the knowledge base for teaching have looked to other sciences as a model for how to codify its current research-based knowledge; the product is a series of abstract summaries of knowledge. Further, these chapters are a distressing parallel to the way many, if not most, teacher education programs have traditionally been organized, that is, as a series of unrelated chapters in methodology, psychology, and foundational and organizational knowledge. Therefore, the KBBT volume appears poised to perpetuate the current structure of teacher education, rather than to serve as a lightning rod for its reform.

Although we are not familiar with parallel texts in other professions, we suspect that a volume like *Gray's Anatomy*, or other similar classic works in medicine, functioned to represent current knowledge—and not a volume entitled *Knowledge Base for the Beginning Physician*. Yet we continue to respect the need for teaching practice thoroughly grounded in an understanding of current research-based knowledge in teaching and learning and used as a guide, but not a prescription, for teaching. However, in our view, teaching is a uniquely human enterprise, and it is this uniqueness that should drive the codification of knowledge and how it will be used by teachers and teacher educators. Consider the following: it is entirely possible to go to a physician and get an accurate diagnosis of the problem without ever having a particularly personal and humanistic interaction with a physician. If he or she is knowledgeable in the abstract, it may be possible to forego the human interaction and even see it as unimportant. The notion of "bedside manner" is for many easily forsaken in exchange for seeing the most highly skilled physician. Not all physicians may agree on whether this is a wise state of affairs, but it is nevertheless the case.

On the contrary, teacher knowledge is always used in a personal context and, to make matters more complex, in a group and societal context as well. This is what makes knowledge for teaching distinct and exciting as well as frustrating for novice teachers who wish absolute answers but must learn to use the absolutes as a guide and not a prescription. The abstract presentation of knowledge, coupled with the separation of topics into the traditional framework which characterizes most teacher education programs, means that the KBBT volume has generally failed to tell the unique story of knowledge for teaching in our contemporary American society to its readers.

In her chapter on "The Ethical Dimension of Teaching," Strom (1989) reminds us that "it is generally recognized that teaching is intrinsically moral" (p. 268). She discusses, in some detail, the need for beginning teachers to engage in deliberations regarding the ethics of their work and ethical dimensions of curricular decisions for example. However, like the balance of the chapters, this particular subject is treated in isolation, apart from the cultural concerns expressed by Cazden and Mehan, Florio-Ruane, and Greene, and makes no mention of the moral dilemma associated with the welfare of minorities in the public education system. Unfortunately, by separating this topic, as others have been similarly separated in the volume, the moral and ethical dimensions of teaching that so sorely need to be addressed throughout a teacher education program appear to be isolated as the province of professors in foundations, rather than an overriding concern throughout programs of teacher education. And the critical relationships between advances in cognitive psychology, which provide guidance for how to address the moral dilemma from the perspective of learners and instruction, are also not drawn.

How would the volume have looked if it had integrated the knowledge we should be drawing on in restructuring teacher education? From the outset it would be clearly distinguished from a purely scientific description of teaching. Therefore, the term "knowledge base" could be seen as a misnomer, and a more appropriate concept might be something like "Guiding the Professional Development of Beginning Teachers." Next, it would be a volume in which each chapter depended on the next for full understanding, and one in which the crucial themes for teaching—instruction, growth and development, the context of schooling, and the nature of contemporary American society—would be prominent throughout. This would summarily preclude a separate treatment of multicultural issues in a stand-alone portion of such a volume. This kind of organizational scheme would mean that the author or authors would be pushed to look, seek out, and examine the linkages between the knowledge they offer and the context in which it would be played out. Finally, it would address the role of research-based knowledge in teaching overtly and provide a clear perspective on its role in learning to teach.

Preparing teachers for contemporary American society is a daunting challenge, but we do, in fact, have more knowledge about teaching, learning, and classrooms to draw on in this effort than ever before. In reconceptualizing how to engage in teacher education, we must take great care to use this opportunity to clarify our unique role, and to stimulate teacher educators to rethink their practice. Clearly, one of the fundamental issues is how we conceptualize effective teaching and learning for the diverse nature of our student population. In the absence of a clear commitment to this issue, knowledge for teaching presented in the abstract will likely fail to provide the groundwork for meeting the needs of today's students in a professionally responsible manner.

■

REFERENCES

Anderson, L. M. (1989). Classroom instruction. In M. C. Reynolds (Ed.), *Knowledge base for the beginning teacher* (pp. 101-115). Oxford, England: Pergamon.

Cazden, C. B., & Mehan, H. (1989). Principles from sociology and anthropology: Context, code, classroom, and culture. In M. C. Reynolds (Ed.), *Knowledge base for the beginning teacher* (pp. 47-57). Oxford, England: Pergamon.

Fenstermacher, G. D (1986). Philosophy of research on teaching: Three aspects. In M.C. Wittrock (Ed.), *Handbook for research on teaching* (pp. 37-49). New York: Macmillan.

Floden, R. E., & Klinzing, H. G. (1990). What can research on teaching thinking contribute to teacher preparation? A second opinion. *Educational Researcher, 19*(4), 15-20.

Florio-Ruane, S. (1989). Social organization of classes and schools. In M. C. Reynolds (Ed.), *Knowledge base for the beginning teacher* (pp. 163-172). Oxford, England: Pergamon.

Greene, M. (1989). Social and political contexts. In M. C. Reynolds (Ed.), *Knowledge base for the beginning teacher* (pp. 143-154). Oxford, England: Pergamon.

Griffin, G. A. (1989). Coda: The knowledge-driven school. In M. C. Reynolds (Ed.), *Knowledge base for the beginning teacher* (pp. 277-286). Oxford, England: Pergamon.

Jackson, P. W. (1986). *The practice of teaching.* New York: Teachers College Press.

McDiarmid, G. W., Ball, D. L., & Anderson, C. W. (1989). Why staying one chapter ahead doesn't really work: Subject-specific pedagogy. In M. C. Reynolds (Ed.), *Knowledge base for the beginning teacher* (pp. 193-205). Oxford, England: Pergamon.

Reynolds, M. C. (1989). Students with special needs. In M. C. Reynolds (Ed.), *Knowledge base for the beginning teacher* (pp. 129-142). Oxford, England: Pergamon.

■   ■

Strom, S. M. (1989). The ethical dimension of teaching. In M. C. Reynolds (Ed.), *Knowledge base for the beginning teacher* (pp. 267-276). Oxford, England: Pergamon.

Tom, A. R., & Valli, L. (1990). Professional knowledge for teachers. In W. R. Houston (Ed.), *Handbook of research on teacher education* (pp. 373-392). New York: Macmillan.

Wang, M. C., & Palincsar, A. S. (1989). Teaching students to assume an active role in their learning. In M. C. Reynolds (Ed.), *Knowledge base for the beginning teacher* (pp. 71-84). Oxford, England: Pergamon.

IDENTIFYING A KNOWLEDGE BASE FOR TEACHING MULTICULTURAL, MULTILINGUAL STUDENTS: AN INTERNATIONAL STUDY

3

LEONARD C. BECKUM, OFELIA GARCIA,

RICARDO OTHEGUY, ARLENE ZIMNY,

ISABELL HOREND, PAULINE PERRY,

ERIC LORD, BRIGITTE ROLLETT

Overview.   One of the greatest challenges in changing the practice of teacher education is preparing teachers to work with multicultural, multilingual populations. The previous chapter noted the absence of sufficient content in the KBBT volume that would be useful in addressing this critical task. This chapter reveals the perceptions of teachers in multicultural, multilingual schools regarding the actual knowledge they use in working with their students on a day-to-day basis. The perception of this group of teachers, drawn from urban areas in three countries, is that attitudes toward children, knowledge of families and communities, and caring about what happens to children are the storehouse of knowledge on which teachers rely when confronted with the challenges of teaching in their particular contexts. The study presented in this chapter further substantiates the importance of knowledge in these areas for beginning teachers, and it also reminds us that working in complex and diverse classrooms sharpens that aspect of teaching that is fundamentally concerned with caring for the children one teaches. ■

It is probable that no educational institution, public or private, is immune from the forces for change sweeping the American educational system. The problem of preparedness, while severe overall, is acute for teachers in urban, poor, multicultural, multilingual, and minority schools. When teachers are less than adequately or inappropriately prepared, both teachers and the children they teach suffer. The impact of this situation is felt in the appalling minority drop-out rate in the United States and in the continuing decline in the pool of minority teachers, from 12% in 1963 to 8% in 1987. It is further anticipated that this number may continue to decline to about 5% by the year 2000 (Wells, 1987). Given the increasingly multicultural American profile, it is very likely that few totally ho-mogeneous bodies of students now exist in our urban or suburban environments–whether the differences be those of ethnicity, culture, or class. How to prepare successful teachers for these diverse populations must be a priority for teacher preparation programs.

While much research has examined effective teaching practices, less has been done to define the knowledge base for teacher preparation, and still less to determine how that knowledge base should respond to the cultural profile of the students or their teachers. Although it has been stated that the begin-ning teacher must understand the relationship between pedagogy and the individual's role in society, this premise still lacks practical pedagogical advice and remains focused on learner-inherent factors rather than teacher-inherent factors. The necessary tie between the teacher's knowledge base and the available informa-tion about student populations and behaviors has yet to be established. Given the high probability that teachers now and in the future will be from the majority cul-ture, research that would determine the relationship between the knowledge of beginning teachers, student characteristics, and the requisites for teaching in a multicultural, multilingual school setting was indicated.

What should constitute the knowledge base for begin-ning teachers working within these differing cultural settings therefore presented an appropriate topic for investigation. Accordingly, this chapter reports on the re-sults of a two-year international case study focusing on the personal, professional, and intellectual characteristics of experienced, successful teachers of minority chil-dren. This particular focus was chosen because although the body of literature on effective teachers in general is vast and growing (Berliner, 1986; Brophy & Good, 1986; Gage, 1978, 1986; Leinhardt & Greeno, 1986; Rosenshine & Stevens, 1986; Shulman, 1978), fewer studies have focused on successful teachers of children from racial and linguistic minorities. The study's aim was to begin to identify the characteristics that contribute to successful teachers of minority children. By identifying the practices and experiences that successful teachers of multiethnic, urban, poor, and multilingual students believe to be responsible for their success, this knowledge may point out lines of development for programs engaged in the preparation of novice teachers to serve populations where children of ethnic or linguistic minorities predominate. These findings would be invaluable for faculty teacher preparation programs involved in restructuring.

■

METHOD

The three institutions that took part in this study were the Universitaet Wien in Vienna, Austria, the London South Bank Polytechnic in England, and the City College of New York in the United States. It was hoped that by learning about effective teachers of children who are similarly situated in that they are part of an ethnic or linguistic minority, but who are from different backgrounds and live in different societies, the study would yield a more general set of conclusions. In this manner, findings regarding characteristics of successful teachers of Black and Latino children in New York City were supplemented by the results of investigations into the characteristics of Afro-Caribbean, Asian, Pakistani, Turkish, and Yugoslavian children in London and Vienna. The study was intentionally limited to elementary schools, for it is during the initial years of contact with the school that children from racial and language minorities go through the period of sharpest transition. The participating schools were located in areas chosen to represent demographic patterns found in each of the cities.

Recommendations for successful teachers who could participate in the study were solicited from the principals and staff of these successful schools. The study thus solicited the participation of 102 teachers, 50 in New York City, 31 in Vienna, and 21 in London. As requested, most of the teachers who were recommended were, in the eyes of their immediate supervisors, not only very successful but also highly experienced. Taking all three cities together, well over 75% of the teachers had been teaching for five years or more at the time of

■   ■   ■

their participation. More than 90% of the teachers were women; the sample contained four men in New York City, three men in London, and two men in Vienna—a proportion fairly representative of the actual distribution of males on elementary school staffs. The ethnicity of the teachers in the European cities was predominantly White, while the American sample was 24% White and 76% Black or Hispanic.

All participating teachers were asked to recall, from the preceding 15 days, two incidents, one which they thought they had handled competently and one where they felt they had not done as well. The teachers were then asked to provide two lengthy statements, one for each incident, reflecting on the personal and professional practices that had made possible the handling of one incident successfully and the other less so. The information gathered by this study, then, comes directly from the teachers' self-reports and, as such, it partakes of all the advantages, and suffers from all the shortcomings, of self-reports. However, one of the aspects that makes this study unique is that its findings are based on the considered introspections of professionals who work in very diverse teaching environments, who are judged by their most immediate supervisors to be obtaining positive results in their teaching of children from minority groups, and who have reflected, in highly concrete terms, on what it is that has made them succeed or fail during recent, specific experiences.

Participating teachers conveyed their reflections concerning the two experiences either in written essays or during taped conversations, depending on the given research team and time constraints in each city. Thus, all statements made by London teachers and some by New York City teachers are in the form of essays, while all Vienna teachers' and the majority of New York City teachers' statements are in the form of transcripts of taped conversations.

In all three cities, the collected statements were subjected to two types of examination, one quantitative and one qualitative. The quantitative examination consisted of a content analysis of topics covered by teachers as they reflected on their positive and negative experiences. The qualitative examinations consisted of a culling of dominant themes, opinions, and remarks that could be used to provide additional insights into the teachers' instructional techniques. These themes have been interspersed throughout the quantitative presentation of the data to complement the quantitative study and to give a full account of the respondents' views on what makes for successful teachers of children from multilingual and multiethnic, urban populations.

On the basis of an initial reading of the essays and the transcripts, a coding manual of 105 topics was developed to subject the data to a systematic content analysis. It bears stressing that these topics were not put forth beforehand but were derived from a careful reading of the statements. The topics are, thus, the respondents' own list of relevant factors that, from their point of view, affect success and failure in the teaching of minority children. All transcripts were coded according to whether there was explicit mention of any one of 105 different content topics, and whether the reference made to the specific topic by the particular informant was of a positive or negative nature. Negative, in this context, does not imply that the teacher's attitude with regard to a particular topic was malicious or prejudicial; a negative topic is simply one that a respondent considered as part of a description of an unresolved or otherwise unsuccessful experience.

FINDINGS

The topics fell into two domains that will be presented separately. The intrinsic domain contains topics that deal with the teachers' own personal and professional characteristics. The extrinsic domain contains topics that deal with factors over which teachers have little direct influence—having to do with communities, institutions, and children. Topics belonging to the intrinsic domain were discussed much more frequently than those belonging to the extrinsic domain. It was also true, in all three cities, that when extrinsic topics were discussed, the general tone was much less positive than when discussion centered on topics belonging to the intrinsic domain.

THE INTRINSIC DOMAIN

This domain contains topics having to do with teacher characteristics and, therefore, is more responsive to the questions initially posed in this study. Overall, the data indicate that the respondents believe that successful teaching results from a combination of knowledge, skill, and organizational capacity, as well as personal and attitudinal qualities. In describing their concept of "the good teacher," the teachers in this study cited such areas of knowledge as information about local communities' familiarity with theories of child development and studies of learning styles, as well as such academic areas as mastery of the subject to be taught. Many also cited such organizational skills as knowing how to arrange children into work groups, being able to provide sufficient space for group activities, allowing children to participate in decision-making, and remaining always conscious of the need to spell out for children the nature of the tasks to be undertaken. Also mentioned were affective elements and personal qualities, such as being able to nurture and love children, knowing how to treat each child as an individual, providing a warm and friendly environment, and remembering to positively reinforce high achievement and good behavior. Finally, many of our respondents cited also their own positive attitudes toward being a teacher.

Affective and Academic Characteristics

The weight teachers gave these variables was highly skewed. It became clear that the factors that the informants regarded as the most important determinants of successful teaching are the affective ones, covering the personal qualities of teachers as well as their attitudes. It was also clear that, in the view of these teachers, organizational skills come in at a close second, along with knowledge of families and community and of the way children learn and develop; academic factors weigh in at a somewhat distant third.

In the view of most respondents, the factor that contributes to successful teaching the most is the ability to build self-esteem and pride in children. This is closely followed by the ability to observe and listen to children and the ability to gain knowledge of individual children. Most of the teachers agreed that a good teacher has to be able, first and foremost, to connect with children and with the profession itself in a manner that is mature, generous, constructive, and sensitive. Most informants spent their time discussing the psychological qualities they possess, as well as the personal-affective moves they make, that lead time and again to successful teaching experiences. For teachers, their belief that affective and personal qualities are more important than academic or organizational ones was demonstrated quantitatively and, as it were, by default. That is, having been given ample opportunity to talk about what made them good teachers, most talked a great deal about the kind of people they are and only a little about the things they know or the academic preparation they have. But some teachers dwelled on these matters explicitly. Typical was this comment by a teacher in New York City:

> It came to me between the 10th and 15th year of teaching. Between the 10th and 15th year of teaching I discovered that what was needed for these children was not an emphasis on the academic but a meaningful interaction with mature adults. The relationship with a stable, mature adult is most important.

This reflection of an experienced teacher highlights the importance of the finding regarding the preeminence of affective factors in her conception of what makes her successful with minority children. It was repeatedly found that it takes a long time for a teacher to feel so comfortable in the teaching-learning situation that she can effectively give attention to these affective factors. In the transcripts, the more experienced teachers were the ones who were able to talk explicitly about the emotional side of life in the classroom.

Another very experienced teacher, who emphasized structure and order, prefaced her remarks by saying: *"Yo siempre le he dado enfasis a la parte afectiva. Lo intelectual viene despues."* ("I've always emphasized the affective part. The intellectual part comes second.") Most of the informants linked the importance of affective factors to the social conditions in which their children live. One teacher's words are typical of this position:

> Teachers are of two kinds, some are just excellent academically and good in teaching techniques. These are only teachers. But there are those of us who have all that, and then put extra effort with those children who are in need. We care and give them love. It all has to do with the target population. In other districts, teachers may not have to be teachers, social workers, and guidance counselors, but in this school you have to be all of the above.

Another teacher echoed her words:

> I've given more attention to the affective part of teaching. Here, more than in a school of upper socioeconomic status, that is important. There are many societal problems. Children are abandoned in terms of the nurturing that once existed.

In a similar vein, another teacher spoke at length of his many years of teaching in the same neighborhood and of his familiarity with the subsequent lives of children he taught. He emphasized that families and communities are often sources of strength for children in his district. But he also stressed the impact that poverty and community disintegration have on many Hispanic and Black children who live surrounded by social problems, of which drug addiction is only the more familiar one. He has found many of the children he teaches are either now in the middle of, or are soon headed for, extremely stressful conditions. He said:

> I think the affective part is more important because I am convinced that what happens academically at the elementary level, does not make any difference at all in the secondary school. . . .What you need to teach in elementary school is the inner strength to overcome the disaster. You can always make up what you didn't learn, even as an adult. But the inner strength has to be given early.

This teacher added that he had seen too many academically successful children who, lacking that strength and despite their good academic skills, ended up on drugs eight years later anyway.

Along these same lines, it should be added that none of the teachers mentioned academic knowledge alone as the determinant of success; that is, all those who mentioned factors relating to the mastery of a discipline spoke at length also of their capabilities as classroom performers. In addition, several teachers explicitly stated their belief that being a good teacher had little or nothing to do with academic knowledge and everything to do with personal qualities. It should be clarified that there is no evidence that these teachers think knowledge and information are irrelevant. They appeared to regard subject matter information as valuable and knowledge, in general, as important. Rather, it seems that though important, academic knowledge and skills are outranked in their estimation by other, even more powerful explanations of teachers' success.

Typical were comments like this: "I care deeply about the children; they're important to me." Another informant's comment on her strengths says:

> My other strength is that I listen to the kids, I listen to their complaints of fear, their uneasiness. I pick it up right away. I am good at picking up nonverbal communication that is often missed. . . .I always hold my breath and listen to the kids. I give opportunity for them to work independently and for me to step back. I give time to the children.

Another teacher answered our question about success in a particular situation completely in children's terms:

> Children were involved in the whole process. Their ideas were considered and esteemed. When a problem arose on my part, the children were informed and included in the solution of it. Honesty on my part in dealing with the children prevailed. I dealt openly with the children about my feelings and needs and what I felt capable of doing and, in turn, respectfully considered their feelings and needs too. . . .In summary, I'd say the bottom line is to trust kids, give them credit. Praise and build their self-esteem

continually. Build a relationship with them where both you and they can feel comfortable and safe in the classroom, safe to be who you are and all you can become.

It seems that this child-centered approach is an important finding regarding the personal orientation of teachers. Their commitment to children is what motivates and inspires their work. These teachers were convinced that all their children could learn and be successful despite their needs when they enter school. This can be most clearly seen from the fact that the content analysis shows the ability to observe and to listen, to know and to work with individual children, as being some of the most important skills these teachers said they possessed. These teachers appear to be successful precisely because they have a special interest in children as individuals. They take the time to listen to them, to observe them, to know them, to know their needs and strengths, and to know what makes them tick and learn.

It seems that when successful teachers encounter children with problems, they do not exclude them from the teaching-learning situation, do not send them to the office, and do not ignore them or call in the parents. Rather, the teacher knows these children well enough to understand how to involve them in a learning situation and how to provide individual students with a situation from which they can benefit. These teachers are confident and self-assured, accommodate their teaching to the learning styles of their students, and never have a condescending attitude. Instead, they trust and respect the ability of all children to learn. The following account of a successful experience with an individual child is perhaps illustrative. This prekindergarten teacher in New York City explained that a certain child had only been in her classroom for a semester and that his concentration was short. She went on to say:

> For the first time he made a helicopter. He was very proud of his helicopter. I wrote down what he said. (Teacher then points to a helicopter that is hanging in the classroom along with a sign. She reads the sign.) It said: 'My father will like this because I finally made something nice.'

These successful teachers seem to know how to build up children's self-esteem so that they can bring them to new heights.

Teacher Orientation to Instruction

Although affective factors, relating to their deep appreciation of themselves as teachers and of children as learners, are reported by the informants as having the most to do with their success, clearly those affective factors do not tell the whole story. In their view, pedagogical skills count for a great deal too. When turning to the craft of teaching, as it is found in the self-reports of these informants, one is immediately struck by what might be described as the democratic climate of their classrooms. By and large, these teachers have classrooms that might seem traditional to the unsophisticated eye, but alternative modes of teaching and learning are taking place. That is, most of these teachers' classrooms may appear physically to be traditional, with desks arranged in the familiar patterns. Yet, the teachers' structure of the teaching situation requires that individual children have some degree of control over their own learning.

Most of the respondents would probably be regarded as traditionalists because they, at times, conduct whole-class lessons. But it is their knowledge of how to deal with children individually and the understanding of how to structure cooperative, small group learning situations that they mention most frequently in connection with the pedagogical skills that contribute to effective teaching. The teachers regarded the ability to teach individual children as most important, the ability to teach small groups second, and the ability to teach the whole class only third. A successful teacher, then, is one who does not always insist on whole-class teaching for all children at all times, and who values most the ability to depart from a whole-class format and attend to the teaching task in a more creative fashion.

In discussing the ways in which they relate to children, these successful teachers made several other important points. Typically, they said they know that children are naturally curious, and they, therefore, try to build their teaching around that curiosity; they know different children learn differently, and they thus teach them in different ways; they know children don't deal in abstractions, and their teaching is, therefore, characterized by presentation of all concepts through concrete experiences.

The following accounts of successful learning situations best illustrate the type of organizational knowledge considered of importance by the respondents. One American teacher wrote about her class's participation in three district projects as follows:

> The first step I took was to tell the students about the idea of working in small groups or committees and about the different projects that they were going to be involved with. I asked them to think about selecting an area of interest as I explained some of the activities that were going to take place in each group and the materials they would be working with. For example, in science, we had been working in small groups, putting electrical circuits together; therefore, the students that were going to be involved in the science-fair group were asked to create an interesting project using the materi-

als and the knowledge they had obtained during the science hands-on activities they had been involved in. . . . .After a preview of the different projects, the students selected a project of their interest. We reviewed the rules of working in small groups. . . .

The next step was to find a large block of time in which the children could work without any interruption. The furniture was arranged during this period to form different work areas to meet the needs of the different groups. . . .The outcome of this situation was very positive. The students involved with the science projects had the opportunity to participate in the school science fair. They demonstrated and shared with other classes in the school what they had learned about electricity.

Another teacher's account included this example:

Two girls who were third graders were given a task of measuring something and selecting what they wanted to measure it by. They decided on the length and width of the room and decided on using yarn. They compared the two yarns. They noticed that one was longer than the other. But I wanted to reinforce the idea of difference, and they just couldn't come up with what the difference between the two yarns was. They struggled with it all week. They had string taped to the floor. It got messed up several times. They kept doing it again. They finally taped where one ended and where the other one ended. Then they noticed that one was different. One was longer. But they couldn't measure the difference. I told them, "Now you know which is which, but I want you to measure the difference."

There was tension, there was conflict. They took the whole week, but it was fine with me. I let them struggle. They started asking the right questions: "How are they different?" And then they finally measured that. It finally clicked. They took an inch tape measure and measured the difference. But they measured incorrectly. Then they came back and told me it was 60. And I said, 60 what? Noodles? They kept going back. With me, clarity is a big thing. They remeasured many times. They started questioning where it really ended, whether the end was the tape or the string. They then told me that there were three 60s. We added and then multiplied; we got 180. We did it with the whole class. Then we did physical graphing with shoes and sneakers.

Although this teacher's account has all the trappings of an open classroom, it can be said that traditional teachers also know how to include the concreteness and the relevance that this open-classroom teacher was addressing. The following account of a successful mathematics lesson came from a traditional fifth-grade teacher in a traditional school setting:

We used raisins to learn about multiplication. There was group participation. Each child was given a box of raisins. They were told to do estimations of how many raisins there were in a box. Some guessed based on the size of each raisin and the size of the box. I told them they could open up the box and look at the top. Based on what they saw, they could give a guess. Each individual child did something different. Some counted the top and then multiplied the rest. Then everyone counted how many raisins were in their box.

We tallied how many got the exact number and ranked the students by order of who had estimated closer to their exact number. Then I grouped them. Each group had to come out with exact, equally divided sets. In this way I taught the concept of division and remainder. They had to figure out how many raisins they had all together, and how many each child would get. This all included a lot of writing, since they had to write down how they had arrived at their conclusion. Then we did sum of totals with different tables. They then had to figure out how to divide equally. This was more abstract; they were asked to answer such things as: If you have 85 raisins, how do you divide them into 12 people?

Of all the items dealing with pedagogical content, the teachers appeared to be particularly eloquent on the matter of concrete versus abstract. They seemed to feel that concrete, hands-on teaching is not only the best but the only way to teach. Most thought that such an approach would lead to success and that those who take the abstract road would meet with failure. When the respondents described things that did not go well in their classrooms, the explanation usually had to do with community factors or with their inability to restrain their temper when faced sometimes with a particularly difficult situation. But, in addition to these explanations for what causes trouble, failure was also generally pinned on abstractness. For example, one of the informants who was eloquent on the fact that children "learn by doing" recalled for us her lack of success at trying to teach children the concept of volume by giving children definitions and having them do problems from a book. "I then figured that they had to build their own containers." Only after elaborate efforts at guiding children through their own construction of containers of different kinds were they able to solve book problems on volume.

The informants also emphasized the importance of good organization, clarity of purpose, and a strong hand. Most of them appeared to believe that good teachers are those able to think clearly about the physical and temporal structure of their teaching and the need of children to understand the shape of their daily schedule, and to grasp the reasons behind the arrangement of the concrete objects and work areas that frame their activities.

Teacher Understanding of the Community

As has been shown, topics having to do with information and knowledge play a relatively minor role in these teachers' perceptions of what makes them successful. The one item of information or knowledge that successful teachers do value greatly is familiarity with the conditions that touch the lives of children outside the school. Good teachers appear to regard of the utmost importance their ability to understand the surrounding community, the resulting capability to connect with parents, and the opening thereby of possibilities to achieve greater insights into the lives of their students. Thus, informants in our sample said they were successful because of the following: They know the specific community where they teach, have mastered from birth its language and culture or have made it a point to acquire this knowledge as an adult, establish good communication with parents and identify with their culture, stress the positive value of the child's ethnicity, are informed about the value of the child's religion, and understand the importance of the child's language.

Some of our informants provided examples of how the complexities of community belongingness impact their teaching practice. One of our Black informants, a teacher at a day-care center, said that children were like adults. "When I go into a room full of White people I freeze up. Then, as soon as I see another Black face I feel it's going to be okay." Children are the same, she said, and she had found that when she taught White children, she had to make an extra effort to show love and concern, to be especially patient, and to give children time to get used to her and to respond. She talked about a recent experience trying to reach two White girls: "I have to reach these children in different ways. Right now, I have to talk first, because this hand, this Black hand (she shows her hand), is not acceptable. It may take some time." The same, she says, takes place in the more unusual situation of White teachers and Black children.

There is no evidence in our transcripts that the teachers feel that the fact of not belonging to the same community as the children is a disabling handicap, but many stressed the enormous advantages that accrue to the teacher who teaches her own. A Black teacher teaching in a predominantly Black prekindergarten said: "The children are more comfortable knowing you're the same color. It's much easier to relate to me because of my blackness, because I'm a female, and because of my age. . . . Color is a definite advantage in dealing with these children." Another Black teacher explained:

> I use what's relevant and familiar to them, especially as Blacks. It's useful that I'm black. It's key to use the African American experience. Not to say that a White teacher cannot do it. But the fact that we're from similar backgrounds enhances my ability. Children need to see African American role models. There are things that are distinct. For example, the language is distinct. And language is very interwoven into every-

■   ■   ■

thing. I know the different ways that African Americans have of expressing something. I know their families, their mothers, their clothing, how the community works,
and how that affects the children's lives. I know what it means to be a Black child, the
traditions that are passed down from one generation to another.

Many minority teachers, and especially the Blacks in the
sample, saw a connection between the advantage of being of the same race and the
issue of upholding higher expectations for Black children. Comments like this one
were typical: "Black teachers give students a positive self-image. . . .Our expectations are different. We know that Black children have inherent intellectual capacities. We demand more. We don't use Black English vernacular as an excuse."
Another Black teacher, who had gone to the same Black school in which she now
teaches, told us:

> I was one of the many Black children who are bright. I see myself in these children. So
> I know I can have very high expectations of my children. I want to see their brightness
> get them somewhere, become a professional. I came to this same school, I sat in these
> classrooms, and I know there's no time to waste.

Yet, none of the minority teachers expressed the feeling that they were the only
ones who could work with minority children. Typical was this comment: "I was
born and raised in East Harlem. You have to feel for this community. If you come
from a different one you could have culture shock. But the important thing is to let
parents teach you about them and their children, and respect all of them."

The teachers recognized, usually quite explicitly, that the
communities many of their children come from have many problems. But they
seemed to be aware, as well, that these communities hold wellsprings of strength
that must be tapped, such as the traditions and ways of speaking that have been
mentioned in previous contexts. Many of the Latino teachers in our American
sample appeared convinced that speaking Spanish is an important part of what
makes them good teachers. And there are accounts in the New York City transcripts, by both Black and White English monolingual teachers, who took the
trouble to learn Spanish so that they could communicate with parents, reinforce
their relationship with the children, and associate themselves with a source of community strength.

More than one of the informants reminisced about their
early years of teaching when they laid down injunctions against the speaking of
Spanish in class, only to reverse themselves after discovering that their policy was

distancing them from the children and the community. One of the White teachers teaching in a mostly Latino school in New York City said:

> When I came to this school, it was my first experience being surrounded by a different language and culture. It was bad enough that I didn't speak Spanish, but it seemed to me that no one spoke English. Being constantly in the dark as to what is being said around you is very nerve-wracking. Since I was a monolingual teacher, I thought I wouldn't have to deal with this in the classroom. I was wrong. Very often the children did speak Spanish. My reaction to this was to banish Spanish from the room. The change in the children was extreme. A noisy class suddenly became silent. If the children didn't know how to say something in English, they said nothing at all.

In the context of the mixture of blessings and difficulties that stem from the child's community, many Black teachers spoke of having to be teacher, social worker, father, and mother to children from very troubled homes. But, as in some of the testimony that has already been recounted, many attribute their success to their own deep familiarity with African American traditions and, in particular, with Southern Black culture. For example, one teacher in a predominantly Black community in New York City stressed how being a member of, and feeling deeply about, the Black community helped her to be a better teacher. She also reflected on community problems. She compared the richly textured culture of the American South with the current situation in New York City. "Many of my children don't know anything about their own background; television does not reflect their culture and leaves them empty and without roots," she said, emphasizing that community links have to be something explicitly taught.

THE EXTRINSIC DOMAIN

The teachers in all cities showed positive regard for the cultural, ethnic, and linguistic diversity of their children's community. Although community resources also received positive mention, only a few teachers talked about them in any detail. In contrast, all other references to the community were negative. Teachers in New York City, for example, found the apparent disintegration of family life, as reflected in a high prevalence of single-parent or no-parent households, as well as drug addiction in the community, to be sources of difficulty, while teachers in London spoke of nonschool-oriented families.

Most of the negative references occurred while the teachers spoke of individual children in their classrooms who were going through difficult times. Typical problematic experiences for American teachers are re-flected in the following examples. Speaking of a girl who needed extra attention, one teacher described:

> The little girl was brought in by her godmother. She was staying with her since her mother was incarcerated. The little girl had been living with the grandmother since the mother was incarcerated. But the grandmother had a stroke and died. There was no father.

Another teacher spoke about the disintegration of the Black community in New York City:

> Education is taking a back seat in the Black community. Maybe it's because of the drugs. The kids see this. They know more than I do. I grew up in South Carolina. This generation is getting worse and worse. The community is relying more and more on schools in order to do what used to be done in the home. For example, kids used to enjoy biblical stories, there was more to look forward to. Now, their idols are the A Team, violence. Religion is absent here. Last year not one child in my class ever went to Sunday school. There are a lot of transient situations, children coming from the hotel nearby. It's different.

Another Black teacher in a school in Harlem adamantly said: "We know the social reasons why the community is like this. The drugs, the distractions in the community, and we don't accept it!"

A typical statement by a London teacher describes a parent-teacher interaction: The parent of an Afro-Caribbean child came to school angry that her son had been reprimanded for being rude to the helpers who supervise school lunch, and she was convinced that he was being picked on because he was black. The teacher knew the mother from previous contacts. She persuaded her to look first at some of the boy's work displayed in the classroom that had earned him praise. The teacher was then able to go on to discuss the behavior that had brought him the reprimand and found the mother willing to talk of similar confrontational behavior that occurred at home that worried her. The teacher believed that her knowledge of the family, and of the difficulties the mother was having, helped her to defuse the situation and to reach an improved relationship with both the mother and the pupil, who was present during the conversation.

Institutional Characteristics

Institutional topics received attention from a relatively small proportion of teachers in New York City and Vienna, while being of virtually no interest to London teachers. Nevertheless, topics dealing with institutional

■   ■   ■

policy seemed to be of greater concern to the respondents than did topics dealing with social conditions of community and family. Moreover, the teachers were more selective in their judgment of institutional items than in their judgment of community conditions. Whereas these successful teachers were, for the most part, very negative about the state of the community, they were selective about criticizing it and recognized their need to understand it if they were to be successful.

The topic that received the most negative criticism dealt with the institutional policy that supports pacing charts and curricular calendars in American schools, followed closely by criticism of special-education evaluation teams. A characteristic comment came from a teacher who explained how the mandated time frames caused chaos in her classroom:

> We were told that each basal reader unit would have to be paced according to guidelines and followed up on a reading chart. . . .My group erupted daily like Mount Saint Helen's. We wrote and reviewed rules of behavior together, but individual children always wanted attention. They called out answers constantly, and soon everyone followed.

It is important to realize, however, that these same teachers were often highly supportive of other mandates. For example, the new science hands-on materials provided by the district, as well as the quantity and quality of other instructional materials that the district made available, earned praise from many of our respondents. This kindergarten teacher's words are typical of the reaction of many of the teachers who spoke to us. Speaking of her love for mathematics and of the district's mandated mathematics curriculum, she said:

> The math curriculum has been good for inexperienced teachers. It is sequential and logical. Before, the math curriculum for kindergarten was informal, there were just goals. Now there's a terrific loose-leaf binder. . . .I like the uniformity of the new math curriculum. It gives me something. I know the goals and the curriculum, but I don't like the things that the children have to do, because they've turned the kindergarten curriculum into a first grade curriculum. I can no longer make chocolate chip cookies and count the chips. It's not possible.

In general, these teachers express anger at the urgency created by the institutional framework. One teacher, who was not under the same constraints as others, expressed it this way:

> If you take the institutional framework, the time requirement is unnatural. . . .If children are given distance, if you let them work with material between them, there is a spark from the material that encourages inquiry. I am always in a dilemma. I work hard to try to do that, to allow the time frame for things to happen. I have to repress

my feelings of urgency about getting things done. Sometimes I get urgent and tense. I lose that relaxed edge that makes me successful.

Conspicuous by its near absence within the accounts of American teachers, excessive class size was a source of difficulty for some teachers in London. At the same time, teachers in Europe and America alike mentioned institutional support systems and the support of their colleagues in a positive light. What seemed to stand out was that these teachers were able to find colleagues who supported and nurtured them. They spoke of sharing knowledge and skills with their fellow teachers. One London teacher said:

> You are not always aware of it, but you learn from the other teachers here. It's not so much because of what they say, but you watch them. You can't help noticing what they do, and you say to yourself: "Yes, that's a better way of doing it."

A teacher in New York City explained her success in the following way: "I am successful because I am good at looking for resources. I do not do things by myself. Everybody puts in *un granito de arena*. Cindy has served as a mentor. We're on the phone constantly." And yet another teacher said:

> My support system in school consists of Dana and her friends. We became friends in the mini-school. There was a common bond. We were Hispanics, women, had similar education, there was a cultural binding. . . .When I want to seek information I know where to get it. I go to classrooms to observe. I take initiative, I follow up, I bother other teachers.

Indeed, the positive value the respondents attached to contact with colleagues was underscored by a negative statement often heard from our informants, namely, the complaint that their schedules did not allow sufficient time to share ideas with other teachers to the degree and with the leisure that they would have wished. The positive views our respondents had of the extent to which they have learned from their colleagues extended, in many cases, to more formal training. Several of our informants mentioned how much they had learned from their college courses, as well as from institutional training sessions.

Student Characteristics

Topics concerning students received varied attention from the teachers in the three cities, with London and Vienna respondents talking about students much more than their American counterparts. In New York City, "students with special emotional needs" was the topic that received the highest number of negative mentions. Similar reactions were recorded by teachers in Vienna, who mentioned that they felt at ease when dealing with instructional tasks, but at times found themselves at a loss when dealing with children who had serious emotional problems. That is, these successful teachers felt most adversely affected in their teaching effectiveness by students with these conditions, and their success lies precisely in the degree to which they can use their own personal and professional characteristics to involve these children, rather than blaming the children for the teacher's lack of effectiveness.

The issue of children with serious emotional problems was deeply felt. In case after case, these teachers portrayed themselves as feeling helpless in front of a child who misbehaved outrageously, or failed totally, and who tended to be regarded by the teachers in the sample as the victim of extremely injurious social and personal circumstances. It appears that many of the informants had devoted enormous amounts of time, energy, and concern to exceedingly troubled children and that most of the time this effort did not get them anywhere. When asked for the story of a failure, it was the pain and frustration associated with these cases that was usually revealed. Teachers felt they wanted to help, wanted to throw themselves into the task of doing something for the child, only to discover that nothing they tried worked.

A successful teacher in New York City told us of her ceaseless efforts to help a child named Angel, who lived with his grandmother in an apartment with no furniture and a single light bulb, whose father was in jail, and whose mother was a drug addict. None of the teachers could help him, but she felt that she understood him and that she would be able to help. She reached out and worked with him. "He was the only child who ever had my personal phone number," she said. His improvement was sporadic. After meeting with endless frustration and working with him without rest, one day he stopped coming to school. He was not in the apartment. He was not in the building. Nobody in the neighborhood could tell her anything about him. He disappeared forever from her life. "I still drive around the neighborhood looking for him," she said.

Interestingly, these successful teachers rarely mentioned children with academic needs. Academic failure seemed to be attributed to a lack of intellectual maturity in the child and, thus, constituted a problem that would solve itself with time. One teacher, speaking of a troubled child whom she couldn't reach, provided some insight into why academic failure was so rarely mentioned by these teachers. "My failure was not with the holdovers. They were immature and needed to stay one more year. But I was a failure as a teacher with this other boy because we just couldn't relate."

■

SUMMARY AND DISCUSSION

It is important in summarizing the findings of this study to restate the principle that influenced the design of the study. The study was based on the belief that successful teachers of multicultural, multilingual, poor children shared some important common beliefs and practices. Secondly, these teachers would most likely describe those beliefs and practices in ways that are unique to them. Lastly, by having these teachers describe their teaching practices, the study could add to the knowledge teacher educators need to develop more appropriate teacher education programs.

The aim of this study was to produce a description of what makes teachers of minority children successful in the view of the practitioners themselves. Because it suffers from obvious limitations relating to the size and nature of the sample, its significance should not be exaggerated. But it should not be understated either, since it represents the opinions of real teachers who were given great freedom to discuss what makes teachers successful.

When discussing their personal characteristics, these teachers describe themselves, in most cases, as individuals of positive qualities who are ideally suited for the job. They attribute their success to the fact that they take children into account when making decisions and to the fact that they like to support children, to encourage them, to guide them, and to help them throughout the day. These qualities appear, as seen through the eyes of the informants, as more of an explanation for their success than even their pedagogical or organizational skills, and considerably more explanatory than knowledge of the material to be taught.

The teachers describe themselves not only as nurturers and lovers, but also as observers and students of children. They say they are successful because they strive to know each child individually. It appears that for these teachers the object of teaching, of learning, and of understanding is each individual child. And even when extrinsic factors such as pacing charts and standardized curriculum impinge on their teaching, they find ways to fashion pedagogical practices to meet the familiar needs of each individual in their classroom.

The informants believe that they are successful because they are expert at their craft—they know how to present material to children so they can assimilate it. These teachers are particularly proud of their flexibility in producing

■ ■ ■

different types of classroom organizations to suit the needs of the moment, of their knowledge of how to organize small work groups, and of their ability to shun abstractions and keep their teaching fastened to a concrete level of tangible objects and materials that children can understand. The respondents ascribe their success to their ability to break away from the mold in order to adapt the teaching-learning situation to children, of whom so much is expected. The typical successful teacher effectively communicates high expectations and professionalism and then places a great deal of trust and responsibility for learning with the children. The ability to develop this demanding and clear, yet democratic climate in the classroom is an important part of what these teachers believe makes them effective teachers. That is, they are effective because they focus on the two important aspects of the teaching-learning process: their skills as teachers and the children's needs and strengths as learners. It appears that the informants develop a learning pact with all children that focuses on children's ability to learn regardless of community, parental, institutional, or psychological factors and that draws on their ability to teach regardless of community, parental, institutional, or psychological factors.

The teachers who were recommended for participation in this study by their principals and colleagues believe that success comes to those who know how to build self-esteem in children, to those who have the ability to observe and listen to individual children and to develop from this an intimate knowledge of each child. Furthermore, the teachers in this study appear to be committed pluralists, with a keen appreciation of racial and linguistic minority characteristics. Traditional customs and values are held in high esteem. When they come from the same communities as their children, they say they know a lot about them. When they come from another community, they endeavor to make the children's community their own, to learn to speak other languages, and to understand people of other races and cultures. They appear to be positive, cooperative, team players—collegial workers who place great emphasis on the academic, intellectual, and emotional support they receive from their colleagues and who wish they could get more of it. The teachers, based on their responses, are enthusiastic optimists who recognize the existence of difficulties and trouble, but attempt to keep it in the world outside and not in their classrooms. The most frequently mentioned positive topic within the extrinsic domain was contact with colleagues.

Obviously, there is a great deal inferred regarding teacher education from what we have learned by asking questions of our experienced professionals. While the teachers in this study cast these qualities as personal characteristics, in reality these characteristics represent goals that should be included in the conceptual framework of teacher education programs. Implicitly, these teachers voiced a philosophy that values a child-centered approach to teaching, ongoing observation of children in classrooms, and the belief that teachers should hold high expectations for all children. These philosophical stances readily translate into identifiable program goals from which explicit preservice experiences can be constructed and examined during the course of teacher preparation.

Shulman (1978) makes the point that teacher performance cannot be understood independently of the subject being taught. While this may be perfectly true, the findings of this study suggest that it cannot be understood independently of community factors, both positive and negative, or even independently of certain key emotional and attitudinal factors either. Teacher education programs, Shulman (1978) suggests, "cannot confine their activities to the content-free domains of pedagogy and supervision." The findings reported here are not at variance with this conclusion, nor do they call for removing these subjects from the discussion. But they do point to the need to include several other subjects besides content and pedagogy. In fact, neither of the two is paramount in the minds of our successful teachers. Pedagogy is regarded as a factor of considerable, but nevertheless of secondary importance, and content figured little in our informants' responses. If any conclusions can be drawn in this regard from such a small and preliminary study—one based on the accounts of real teachers—it is that teacher education programs cannot confine their activities to the emotion-free domains of content, pedagogy, or supervision. Teacher education programs must include community and affective considerations that our successful teachers regard as primary. Until this content is integrated into teacher education programs, we will not have achieved a complete knowledge base for teaching.

REFERENCES

Berliner, D. (1986). In pursuit of the expert pedagogue. *Educational Researcher*, *15*, 5-13.

Brophy, J. E., & Good, T. (1986). Teacher behavior and student achievement. In M. C. Wittrock (Ed.), *Handbook of research on teaching* (3rd ed., pp. 328-375). New York: Macmillan.

Gage, N. L. (1978). *The scientific basis of the art of teaching*. New York: Teachers College Press.

Gage, N. L. (1986). *Hard gains in the soft sciences: The case of pedagogy*. Bloomington, IN: Phi Delta Kappa.

Leinhardt, G., & Greeno, J. G. (1986). The cognitive skill of teaching. *Journal of Educational Psychology*, *78*, 75-95.

Rosenshine, B., & Stevens, R. S. (1986). Teaching functions. In M. C. Wittrock (Ed.), *Handbook of research on teaching* (3rd ed., pp. 376-391). New York: Macmillan.

Shulman, L. (1978). *Investigations of mathematics teaching: A perspective and critique*. Unpublished report, Michigan State University, Institute for Research on Teaching.

Wells, A. S. (1987, April 12). Wanted, 1 million school teachers. *The New York Times*, Education Life, Section 12.

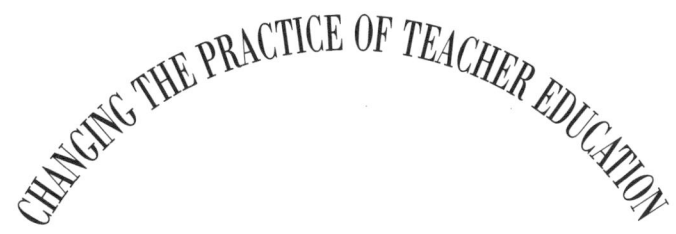

ALTERNATIVE CONCEPTIONS OF ACADEMIC KNOWLEDGE FOR PROSPECTIVE ELEMENTARY TEACHERS

4

FRANK B. MURRAY

Overview. If reform in teacher education is to succeed, change will have to extend beyond what takes place in the professional phase of preparation to include how knowledge is delivered in the traditional liberal arts component that makes up a large portion of teacher education. In this chapter, the role of the liberal arts is explored, particularly as it relates to preparing prospective elementary teachers, and then six alternative conceptions of liberal arts study are posed. If the liberal arts are to inform teachers' understanding of their work, as well as to provide the content on which they draw for their instruction, teacher educators will have to engage in ongoing dialogue with their peers in liberal arts as a central part of their reform efforts. Chapter 8 of this volume describes one instance of the kind of dialogue that can take place when, as Murray encourages us to do in this chapter, we begin to explore the reform in consultation with our colleagues in the liberal arts. ■

This chapter draws heavily on the work of Project 30, a project directed by Daniel Fallon and Frank Murray and supported by Carnegie Corporation of New York.

Everyone agrees, whether they are reform minded or not, that teachers—regardless of what else they study—must study the liberal arts because the liberal arts are somehow thought to be an indispensable component of teacher education programs. Some have gone so far as to argue that the liberal arts should be the only component of the teacher education program. Curiously, almost no one attempts, in any of the reform reports, to specify what the liberal arts are—how many there are, for example, what domains of knowledge are represented, what is essential, and what makes the study of some things liberal and others something else. As the historical record will show, a liberal arts education has been about very different things at different times. How can teacher educators respond with confidence to the universal call to base the education of teachers on a firm, perhaps even an exclusive, education in the liberal arts?

How, in fact, is the teacher's or the pupil's education served by the teacher's knowledge of the liberal arts, as opposed to the other forms of knowledge? If the teacher knows his or her subject matter and, by virtue of a good general education, is reasonably well-informed about other matters, what else can the liberal arts contribute to the teacher's work?

■

THE LIBERAL ARTS TRADITIONS

There are two distinct traditions of liberal arts education. One is the orator tradition, the historical antecedent of the contemporary liberal arts, in which the teacher learns to speak the truth eloquently about the best and most noble of what is known, so that the pupils will act virtuously and govern themselves wisely. The other is the philosopher tradition, the intellectual antecedent of the contemporary view of the liberal arts, in which the teacher's, and subsequently the student's, honest and unending pursuit of truth is the outcome of a liberal education. The orator tradition has been undervalued in contemporary higher education, but the two traditions are nevertheless parts of a whole, in the same sense that the Greek concept, logos, binds together the concepts of speech (oratio) and reason (ratio). It may not be important, in the end, to worry too much about

■   ■   ■   ■

whether teacher education should be anchored to one or the other tradition; each is as much an implication of the other since telling the truth implies having searched for the truth, and searching for the truth is either impossible, or pointless if the search remains unexpressed.

Even so, regardless of the confusion about the exact nature of the liberal arts, what is the unique contribution of the liberal arts to teacher education? The claim that teaching is a profession, and not merely an occupation informed by precise rules and procedures for accomplishing the desired outcomes, stems from the fact that the teacher must rely on other bodies of knowledge, besides pedagogy and teaching technique, to teach well. The nature of these "other bodies" of knowledge and their connection to the classic liberal arts is a difficult problem for teacher educators and nearly everyone else. While the content of the liberal course of study may appear to be arbitrary, its outcome is not—it must take even the successful teacher beyond technique and algorithms, and this is its unique role in all professional education.

Thus, the liberal arts component of the teacher education program must deliver at least three things:

- the subject matter knowledge for which the teacher is directly responsible in the classroom;

- the general education knowledge that defines what the well-informed person knows, apart from the knowledge and information the teacher is responsible for directly conveying to pupils; and

- a kind of knowledge that also does not appear ever to be directly taught to any pupil, but which is thought to be very useful all the same. This knowledge is alleged to provide the teacher with the set of attitudes and dispositions enumerated in the next section. These permit the teacher to go beyond teaching technique.

■

CLAIMS FOR THE CENTRALITY
OF THE LIBERAL ARTS

Sometimes the claim for the importance of the liberal arts for teacher education is made on the grounds that teachers simply ought to be well-educated persons, and well-educated persons are those, and only those, who were schooled in the liberal arts. There is confusion here because being well-educated is often taken as merely being well-informed, and being well-informed is not the same thing as being liberally educated. While general education and liberal education are often taken to be about the same things, they are really about different things—the one being about having good and dependable information, and the other about knowing what the point of something is, and what is worth doing. The issue of general and liberal education must each be explicitly addressed in the liberal arts component of the teacher education program.

The case for subject matter knowledge is conceded by everyone, and nearly everyone has discovered that the traditional college major in the subject matter is rarely adequate preparation for the prospective teacher in this regard. The general knowledge component, by all accounts, enhances the teacher's image as an educated person, but as the material is not required to be taught directly, the benefits to the pupil are not immediately apparent. Consequently, the case for general knowledge has to be made carefully because its role is contested on the grounds of whose culture should provide the general context for schooling and curriculum.

The claims for the distinctly liberal aspects of the liberal arts, while they appear distant and somewhat arbitrary, are actually quite practical because they aim to help the teacher go beyond technique. Thus, in addition to guaranteeing that teachers know their subjects, the liberal arts portion of the curriculum has these additional attributes:

■ They are those subjects that are worth knowing for their own sake; they are ends in themselves, activities that make human life complete.

■ They are studies that are appropriate for the free person, the person who is free of utilitarian concerns, free from the need of labor; in other words, they are studies that are appropriate for leisure.

■ ■ ■ ■

■ They are studies that promote the full realization of what it means to be human and intelligent, that support the selection of wise and good ends for the community and oneself.

■ They are studies that set the student free—free from the bondage of convention, unanalyzed custom and opinion, free of the tyranny of dogma and assertion, and free to search out and construct truth.

■ They are studies that make a difference when they are expressed; they have an effect of persuading others to take up virtuous and just courses of action, and they yield good citizens who can lead the society wisely and to good ends.

■ They are studies that show the student how, by the power of human reason, to search for and construct truth—truths not heretofore known and, truths, owing to the diversity in human reason and perspective, that are inevitably provisional because all the thinkers have not, and cannot have, completed their work.

■ They are studies that enable one to tell the truth eloquently about the most durable and best of what we have learned.

More importantly, these studies should confer certain attitudes and dispositions on those who study them. Among these is an attitude of freedom from *a priori* constraints and assertions; a belief in the centrality and efficacy of the intellect and power of reason; a pervasive skepticism about any answer being a final answer; a tolerance of contrary views and positions; an egalitarianism of thinkers and learners; an overriding—and perhaps misplaced—value on individual autonomy, development, and accomplishment; and the sense that the pursuit and construction of truth—even the truth about the liberal arts—is more important in the end than the discovery of the truth, because truth is always provisional, awaiting the results of subsequent investigations and analyses, and contingent on the experiences and actions of the full range of students and investigators. Finally, there is the sentiment that truth is vast, beyond the competence of an individual mind to construct and comprehend, and, thus, genuine understanding requires the dialectical confrontation with the full historical and contemporary community of thinkers.

This issue of the diversity of cultural and intellectual perspectives in the complete community of thinkers is not a peripheral matter or a desirable add-on in liberal arts education; the issue is at the heart of the reform of the courses of study, in both education and the arts and sciences. How could it be otherwise when it is the honesty and accuracy of the curriculum that is at stake? The charge that higher education is parochial and insensitive to international and global matters, as well as to matters of significance to the nation's many minority groups, is fundamentally a charge that the curriculum is wrong, the very thing it cannot be!

All claims made in the curriculum must be qualified by confirmed scholarship on race, ethnicity, gender, and cultural perspective. We see, for example, that the claims for a monolithic western civilization need to be qualified by any number of facts: Beethoven's ninth symphony contains Turkish marches; statues of Buddha are found in Viking graves; mosques become churches and back again; and like the northern rim, the southern and eastern rim of the Mediterranean Sea contributed to the canon. We mislead our students when we leave out the facts that early Africans were using iron while the early Europeans were using stone, that learning centers existed at Timbuktu and Sankore at the time of the beginnings of the great European universities, or that science and mathematics flourished in the Orient, South America, and Africa before the Greeks and Romans codified their parts of these disciplines.

The point is that the study of minority issues or the study of global or international issues will fail, as they have in the past, if they are not anchored, passionately and with conviction, in the core values of the academy. Attempts to secure a place for these matters in federal law and regulation, in arguments about compensation for past injustice, in assertions about fairness and decency, in appeals to the specter of failure in the international markets, or in the realization that minorities can exert political power over the allocation of public dollars may produce short-term gains. They will fail ultimately to win a place for cultural diversity in higher education, however, because the effort can be deflected so easily by its critics when it is based on these short-term considerations and arguments. Moreover, the diversity in the educational history of the various American minority groups is too complex and inconsistent for such an approach.

The one sure anchor for international education and the study of cultural diversity in teacher education is the core value of the academy, namely the pursuit of truth. The odds for success in this pursuit, for truth yielding its secrets, go up significantly when multiple perspectives are brought to bear in the search. At each stage of cognitive development, moreover, an individual's cognitive growth is enhanced by the confrontation of divergent views, by the clash of paradigms and theories.

In summary, the liberal arts component of the elementary education program must make a provision for the following:

- *Subject Matter Understanding.* How should teachers acquire a thorough knowledge of the discipline(s) they are licensed to teach? Six approaches will be proposed. The traditional college major in the teaching field provides insufficient preparation. The structure and purpose of the academic major need to be rethought anyway, but especially as it applies to teachers.

- *General and Liberal Knowledge.* How do teacher education graduates become well-informed persons? The core curriculum or general education curriculum is usually insufficient by itself to strengthen this essential component of professional standing in prospective teachers. Beyond being well-informed, however, teachers must have the habits of mind that have always been claimed for a liberal education if they are to become more than teaching technicians.

- *Pedagogical Content Knowledge.* How do teacher education students learn how to convert their knowledge of the subject matter into a teachable subject for a wide range of pupils? This is the weakest link in teacher education programs and the area that requires the most intense and lively cooperation between faculties in education and in the arts and sciences.

- *Multicultural, International, and Other Human Perspectives.* For all persons, but especially for prospective teachers, the college curriculum must be accurate with respect to recent scholarship on matters of race, gender, ethnicity, and cultural perspective. This is, of course, a massive undertaking in view of the fact that most higher education faculty were educated in a period when there was very little sensitivity to, or awareness of, alternative perspectives in each curricular domain.

■

THE EDUCATIONAL FOUNDATIONS COMPONENT

It is not widely appreciated that the so-called foundations courses in teacher education are functionally part of the liberal arts component. Rarely are these courses perceived as having direct relevance for the classroom, and they are, therefore, often criticized by teacher education students and teachers in the field. It is a misguided criticism, however, because these courses offer explanations of schooling, not prescriptions or remedies for schooling. Their function in the teacher education program is the same as the claims made for the function of the liberal arts, and they should be held, as a result, to the same expectations we hold for the liberal arts component.

The knowledge of educational foundations is really the knowledge teachers might have used, or could have used, to explain and justify their performance in teaching. It is the teacher's literacy in fields including educational history, philosophy, sociology, psychology, and research, and this knowledge ought to play a role in the teacher's thinking, whether or not it actually plays a role in the teacher's performance.

Thus, to establish that teachers could have, might have, or even should have, based their teaching performance on some knowledge of the foundation disciplines of education, or some body of research literature, is of course no evidence that they did, or would ever, base their performance on that knowledge. Consequently, any effort to measure teachers' knowledge of the educational foundations literature, or the research literature on effective teaching practices, could prove to be irrelevant because the expert teacher, like the fluent speaker, undoubtedly based performance on some area of competence other than the formal knowledge of the academic discipline that might have, or could have, supported the teacher's or speaker's expert performance.

It is essential, therefore, to base the instruction in educational foundations on the knowledge teachers would actually use in their performance—unless, of course, the goal of instruction is literacy for its own sake, whether or not it does indeed influence what teachers do when they teach. There are many reasons why it would be good to have teachers who are literate in the

■   ■   ■   ■

discipline (or disciplines) of education, of course, but the primary goal in teacher education is to have students acquire that mixture of knowledge, skill, and disposition that truly affects what teachers do.

Unfortunately, we are just beginning to explore how teachers actually think about their teaching, and how that knowledge is developed. In this context, educational foundations knowledge can provide teachers with reasons for doing what they do, and instruction in the foundations disciplines should be about the explanations of common schooling phenomena. The core of instruction in the foundations should be tied to generic teaching dilemmas or cases, covering any or all of the foundations disciplines, that could be posed in a way to promote the development of a mature structure of reasoning about teaching and schooling. In the end it is the cognitive structure that is important, not the specific content or information, but rather its form and adequacy. The success of instruction in the educational foundations is measured by how well teachers understand and explain any professional problem or event.

Given that so much rests on teachers' ways of thinking about schooling, there is a need to be sure that teachers can evaluate evidence, can spot a fad or an unsound proposal for innovation, have an educated view of how the pupil's mind develops, have a reasoned and informed position on the major public policy issues that affect schooling, and so forth. On what reserve do the teachers draw when they face a novel problem? Surely, teachers ought to have acquired more than a pop-psychological view of how the mind works, or a pop-sociological view of how, for example, families, schools, and cultures thrive. Amateurs make bad guesses and predictions, and they have no defenses against destructive educational fads because common sense and folk wisdom only work in the easy cases.

THE ACADEMIC MAJOR
FOR ELEMENTARY EDUCATION

The typical academic major and the general group requirements in higher education, while valuable as graduate school prerequisites or for entry level employment, do not deliver currently what is needed for teachers, as will be apparent shortly. In addition, the liberal arts curriculum, if it is to accomplish any of its goals, must be accurate overall. But, as we have seen in the foregoing sections of this chapter, it must be accurate where at the moment it is vulnerable, namely, with respect to recent scholarship on race, gender, and cultural perspective.

Obviously teachers must know the very subject matter they hope to teach their pupils so that regardless of what other claims are made for a liberal education, there must be firm guarantees that teachers understand the very subjects they propose to teach. Yet, in the case of elementary teachers, we are hard-pressed to follow the implications of what we believe very far, because it would mean that prospective elementary teachers would need to be well-grounded in mathematics, literature, writing, history, geography, the natural and social sciences, the fine arts, language, and much more. What kind of academic course of study could ever lead to such an outcome in today's university—for anyone, let alone education students?

On the face of it, the academic major in any one of these fields cannot be the solution to this problem because it does nothing for the teaching of the other mandatory elementary school subjects. The attempt to departmentalize the elementary school is advocated as a prerequisite step in solving this problem because then a single academic major might make some sense as the mainstay of teachers' preparation. Departmentalization in the elementary school, however, has several drawbacks, one of which is that the pupil does not see an adult integrate the knowledge the pupil must come to integrate and bring to bear on the problems of childhood. One wants to see the pupil develop the confidence to attack any problem intellectually and reason about it in a productive and appropriate manner; the teacher should be able to do this with regard to the same academic subjects and problems. Consequently, the single academic major, as the main element in the reform of elementary teacher education, is not likely to lead to improved schooling. As we shall see, the traditional major will not yield the kind of understanding the teacher needs in any case for two reasons. First, the traditional major ignores the other essential subjects in the curriculum. Secondly, departmentalization or specialization in the elementary curriculum, while it would legitimize specialization in the teacher's preparation, works against the critical integration of knowledge and skills and sets a bad example for the pupils. Departmentalization provides a bad example because it promotes the idea that a significant person, like the teacher, can disregard and be disinterested in certain portions of the elementary school curriculum at a time when the modern person cannot ignore any of these areas or be complacent about avoiding certain types of thinking. The problems of our modern world require multiple approaches and perspectives that presume literacy in language, natural and social science, mathematics, aesthetics, and so on.

How, in fact, do elementary teachers come to know the material they teach and, given the latitude in the elementary school curriculum, how do teachers even figure out what that material should be? We do know that reasonably well-educated college and university graduates find themselves in great difficulty early on in their attempts to answer coherently and with integrity the questions that young children are likely to put to them. Sooner or later, for example, elementary teachers, regardless of their college major, are going to tell children that the world, despite all appearances, is not flat. On learning that the earth is round and spinning, children will inevitably wonder why they don't fall off. Teachers, and virtually all educated persons, will say something about the holding power of gravity, and having said that, they will have nearly exhausted all they know about this topic. They have no intellectual resources left to deal with other questions about gravity, such as whether gravity is stronger on the earth's bottom where it presumably has to do so much more work to keep everyone from falling off. In fact, there is some risk, when teachers are pressed to say more about what gravity is, that pupils will be told that gravity is a magnetic force, which it is not; thus, the pupils are misled about a point that will need to be corrected later if the pupils are to have even a rudimentary grasp of how the universe operates.

Even more to the point is the case of a recent National Science Foundation video in which some of Harvard's graduating seniors were asked at their commencement how it is that we have seasons. Without hesitation and with confidence they each replied incorrectly that it was because the earth was closer to the sun in the summer and farther away in the winter. Yet each would, no doubt, know the distance between the earth and sun, that daylight is of different duration throughout the year, the shape of the earth's orbit, that the seasons differ by hemisphere, and so on—all facts, which on reflection, are inconsistent with their response. The point is that the nation's best and brightest are not themselves well grounded in an essential but relatively simple part of the elementary school curriculum. And it would not be hard to document that gaps like this exist among our best and brightest in all aspects of the elementary school curriculum! Given this outcome, what hope is there for the elementary education major—who is typically not a high scorer on any of the common standardized measures of intellectual aptitude and achievement—to master even the subject matters of the grade in which they expect to teach? What kind of education could provide the grounding in the basic subject matters that would allow teachers to stand up to the ordinary questions they will receive from their pupils, let alone the exotic questions they will receive that would tax scholars in the field? How often can teachers simply say, "Good question, look it up," before they discourage all genuine questions from their pupils?

SIX APPROACHES TO THE ELEMENTARY EDUCATION ACADEMIC MAJOR

Six approaches to the question of the elementary academic major are presented, none of which are mutually exclusive. The final outcome could well have features from each approach within an interdisciplinary major option that is discussed below.

1. INTERDISCIPLINARY MAJOR

The major is actually a collection of reworked minors in six areas of the elementary school curriculum—mathematics, foreign language, history and social science, English and language arts, natural science, and fine arts. Each "minor" would have to be responsive to the unique requirements of the elementary school teacher insofar as each could have courses tailored to the needs of the elementary school teacher, either through the integration of the methods courses or by the addition of special sections of subject matter courses that would treat pedagogical issues. The interdisciplinary major option is fairly conservative and administratively feasible. It represents about 90 credit hours of focused study. This option mandates a significant increase in the current elementary teacher education programs but still affords only minimal levels of study in each area. Yet it is an honest approach insofar as each major area of the elementary school curriculum can be addressed in a coherent manner.

The basis for coherence in the interdisciplinary approach is found in each of five remaining themes, by which the separate minors could be reshaped with the interests of the prospective elementary school teacher in mind.

2. PHILOSOPHY OF SUBJECT MATTER

In this approach the philosophy of each subject matter (e.g., philosophy of science) is taken up, and essential and fundamental aspects of the structure of subject matter are covered. Elementary science instruction, for example, would be improved if teachers understood that there are no facts apart from theories, or that "true" theories are not those that were proved but only those that have failed to be disproved. Similarly, social studies education would be improved if teachers would view the history curriculum not so much as the recreation of the past but as one of several possible stories of the past that could be constructed to make sense of the same historical events. The barriers to an understanding of mathematics would be lower if teachers appreciated the similarities in the grammar and syntax of mathematics and language, and so on.

This approach is related to the "structure of the disciplines" approach to curriculum reform that followed the Sputnik educational crisis some 25 years ago. The underlying coherent principles or structures that hold academic disciplines together are the subject of the courses themselves. The separate natural sciences, for example, can be organized by the principle of evolution (evolution of species, matter, solar systems, societies and cultures, sub-atomic particles, chemical reactions), or by the principle of orders of magnitude (e.g., the powers of ten device of relating sub-atomic structure, biochemistry, and celestial systems, as well as the design constraints of other physical and animate structures that stem from their size alone).

3. TEXT APPROACH

This approach entails a close reading of seminal texts (the "great books") in each area, coupled with an examination of school textbooks, for the assumptions each makes about the discipline in question. The logic of this approach, like the philosophy of the disciplines approach, is that the core structure of each discipline is addressed directly by the initial promulgator of an idea. The promulgator, like the teacher, also took on the burden of making ideas clear to an audience who, like the classroom of pupils heard them for the first time. The teacher's grasp of the origins of important ideas may provide a good foundation for the teaching of these ideas to pupils who come to them for the first time. This approach is not to be confused with the discredited "cultural epoch" approach to curriculum and pedagogy, in which the mental development of young pupils was thought to recapitulate the race's cultural and intellectual history.

4. GENETIC EPISTEMOLOGY

This option entails the study of the developmental parallel literature from the perspective of the development of the concepts that make up the curriculum. This approach teaches students the relevant developmental constraints on the pupil's acquisition of the curriculum and lays out, as an unavoidable part of the discussion, the nature of the subject itself. The story of how the young child develops the notion of number, for example, is valuable in its own right, but also reveals salient portions of number theory, the arithmetical algorithms, and other aspects of mathematics. Similarly, the account of the child's moral development reveals the principal issues in moral philosophy and political theory, for example.

It would not be possible to study the development of the child's concept of weight, for instance, without studying the same notion as it appears in Newtonian mechanics and other branches of physics. The young child can be shown to operate with the following "equation" for weight:

Weight = f [the object's mass, size, shape, texture,
temperature, hardness, continuity, and
label but not the object's horizontal or
vertical position in space]

The elementary school teacher needs to be aware of the young child's view of weight because it is based on a consistent child-logic that has implications for pedagogy and curriculum design.

■   ■   ■   ■

Adolescents and many adults operate with a simpler and, to some degree, more sophisticated "equation" as far as it goes.

Weight = f [the object's mass]

In other words, the only way adults can think of to change an object's weight is to alter its mass, that is, add something or take something away from the object. The young child can imagine many other ways, all unfortunately incorrect, for altering weight. The educated person operates with another expression, viz.

Weight = f [mass of the object x mass of the planet/
square of the distance between their
centers]

In addition, the educated person may be able to convert the expression into a genuine equation via a value, [g], for the gravitational constant that permits algebraic manipulation of the terms in the expression. At this point other factors may be introduced into the expression to treat certain buoyant forces or the earth's variation in g, and so forth. To understand the development of the child's thought entails the consideration of the developmental endpoint of the concept or the way the concept might be represented in the curriculum.

There is a similar developmental progression for the child's understanding of the beam balance, in which the young child's understanding of "weighing" is controlled solely by the effects of adding or subtracting weight from a beam balance pan without the influence of any other factor. Later the distance of the balance pan from the fulcrum is gradually factored into the child's scheme for the operation of the balance, and after several more developmental steps we see the product moment law in place in the adolescent's thinking. All concepts and relations in the curriculum can be profitably approached from this perspective. The approach also has face validity because it contains the kinds of information that prospective teachers accept as clearly relevant for their future work.

5. COGNITIVE PSYCHOLOGY

While a developmental approach is naturally appealing for elementary teachers, the student teacher could just as easily major in cognitive psychology and make the workings of the mind a specialization. As in the developmental approach, the subject matter content would be picked up through the consideration of how the mind operates mathematically, aesthetically, and so forth. Like the philosophy of the disciplines or text approaches, this approach would provide a structure for the reformed minors in each subject area. Each area would be approached from the perspective of how we think about and know the content in question. The approach fits well with the current trend in cognitive psychology that stresses the domain specificity of our thinking as opposed to general laws of learning and thinking that transcend particular contexts and situations. Thus, it is not possible in modern psychology to avoid considering the subject matter specifics of what the psychological subject is being asked to learn, discover, remember, utilize, and so forth.

6. PEDAGOGICAL CONTENT KNOWLEDGE

This approach addresses the fact that teachers, even professors, inevitably transform what they know into a teachable subject. They give the subject a new structure and meaning, one that is appropriate to their students' level of understanding. How, in other words, are academic disciplines transformed into school lessons?

All teachers know that the subject matter they teach is different from the subject matter they learned from their own teachers. The knowledge that supports this conversion of the storehouse of knowledge into the school curriculum, into something that has meaning for the pupil, is what is meant by the expression, pedagogical content knowledge.

Education critics often say that, owing to the low quality of teaching, students at both the school and university level are driven to memorize by rote large portions of the curriculum, with the point of education being little more than to return this rotely memorized and undigested material to the teacher on an examination. However, we know that the human mind cannot memorize very much material by rote, in fact probably not much more than half dozen unrelated items at a time. We know that even the marginal pupil who confronts the massive amounts of material in the school and university curriculum finds a way to impose some structure or some organizational scheme on the material. The question is never whether there was some structure, theory, or scheme, but only whether the structure was good or poor. Whatever the teacher actually did in the lesson, the pupils will find some way to make sense of it, to code it, to assimilate it into what they already know, often with an outcome the teacher may never have intended. The nearly universal "error" by which pupils mistake Martin Luther King for Martin Luther in the world history class is just one of a thousand examples, many quite humorous, of pupils' often desperate attempts to make sense of what is presented by the teacher.

The discussion of pedagogical content knowledge is a discussion of the appropriate ways of organizing information and knowledge. It is the search for structures, ways of representing the subject matter, analogies and metaphors that will take each pupil well beyond what can be held together temporally and spatially through rote memorization. At the lowest pedagogical content knowledge level, there are mnemonic structures that can carry the student past the half-dozen rotely memorized items, but these structures accomplish very little other than improving retention and defending the memorized items against the rapid forgetting that is the hallmark of most rotely learned material. The mnemonic device, "roygbiv" can provide the student with the order of the spectral colors. Like all mnemonic devices, however, it fails to provide understanding—it gives no clue about how or why the phenomenon takes place, or why the order is reversed in the second rainbow of a double set, for instance. Knowing the order of the colors can be very helpful and may be essential information for the solution to many higher order problems, but we want more than this. Pedagogical content knowledge is fundamentally about those structures that confer some appropriate level of understanding, and it is ultimately focused on those structures that actually advance our understanding.

Discussions of pedagogical content knowledge are at the heart of professional educators' work and cannot be avoided. We know that the young elementary school child will be taught one of the algorithms for subtraction—but which one, decomposition, equal additions, or the rule of nine is pedagogically and academically sensible? The matter must be, and will be, decided. Similarly, we know that we will teach *Hamlet* at some point, but how should it be represented, and what do we claim it is about—the use of language to talk about language, the pathology of indecision, the unconscious mind of the adolescent, or the recreation of an historical event?

These pedagogical content structures can be studied and codified. Since this reformulation of the discipline is inevitable, one might as well address it directly and, as in the other approaches, use it as a way to structure the reformed minors. In teaching *Huckleberry Finn*, for example, the teacher inevitably interprets the book as a story of race relations, or generation gaps, or an historical period, or latent homosexuality on the frontier, or whatever. How is this done, and shouldn't the academic major address this question explicitly?

As another example, many science teachers attempt to clarify the nature of electric current by comparing it to the behavior of water currents in various sized pipes. Is this a good way to think about electricity, and how would one know? The answer to the question is not to be found in physics nor in education but in a qualitatively different kind of knowledge that will come from conversations between disciplinarians and pedagogues. This knowledge—the knowledge of what is a telling example, a good analogy, a provocative question, a compelling theme—is a proper object of study in an academic major and could yield the kind of understanding of the disciplines that is deep and generative. To have multiple ways of representing a subject matter, to have more than one example or metaphor, to have more than one mode of explanation, requires a high order and demanding form of subject matter understanding.

We need to enrich the discussion of pedagogical content knowledge with the notion that some structures are scaffolds, and as scaffolds, they are provisional and designed solely to advance the pupil to another place. Thus, it may be appropriate to introduce the *1812 Overture*, and by implication all classical music, as the recreation of an event, as programme music, in which the two national anthems battle each other in the overture as the armies did on the battlefield. This representation, or structure, which is hopelessly inadequate for any later understanding of musical composition, may provide a beginning scaffold that will engage the pupil. In the teaching of descriptive statistics, for example, it may make sense to introduce the notions of central tendency and variation with physical models of equilibrium, or with computer graphics representations of data points, or as calculation formulae, or as the solution to certain questions in the behavioral sciences, or as derivations of algebraic equations, or as part of a system of expressions in calculus or some other branch of mathematics. These pedagogical options merit study by an approach that is as serious as the approach to any question in any academic discipline.

A few have seen that this kind of knowledge advances the academic discipline itself. At the cutting edge of a discipline, pedagogical content knowledge and theoretical breakthrough may be the same thing. What happens on the frontiers of a discipline? The researchers invent ways to communicate with each other about the phenomenon under study; they invent ways to make sense of the phenomenon. The "double helix," for example, was as much pedagogical content knowledge as a Nobel Prize winning description because it provided a means for researchers to teach each other, to converse about the genetic code.

When teachers invent a structure that organizes and gives meaning to a field of study, they are doing exactly what the scholars or researchers do when they provide a novel or generative structure for their peers about some problem in their field. Thus, the study of pedagogical content knowledge can be a study on the cutting edge of a field, insofar as new modes of representing the subject matter and new ways of making it interesting and meaningful are formulated.

CONCLUSION

Each of these approaches to the organization of an inter-disciplinary major for prospective elementary teachers addresses the question of how teachers are to learn and understand the subjects they will teach. This question is also central for liberal arts faculty planning academic majors for students aspiring to nonteaching careers. By way of addressing many of the problems inherent in the typical academic major, higher education reformers have recently advocated the creation of capstone courses or senior seminars in each academic major. These courses would integrate the content of the major, show how the major course of study is related to other domains of knowledge, and rescue the current academic major from its vocational character and infuse it with the values claimed for the liberal arts.

The development of such courses naturally entails many of the issues covered in the six approaches to the problem of the elementary academic major. Each approach could provide a way to organize these capstone events. For example, the study of the school curriculum, K-12, would offer a compelling way to structure a capstone course because it demands that the "capstone" aspects of each discipline be confronted and examined. There is hardly an issue in mathematics, for example, that is not addressed directly in the design of the K-12 mathematics curriculum because the core structure of the discipline of mathematics, the very thing the capstone course is about, must be confronted in the design of the K-12 curriculum. Whatever holds the K-12 curriculum together holds the discipline itself together. In this way, education, as an academic discipline, can provide a reciprocal service to the reform of the liberal arts majors in higher education.

CHALLENGES

TO

CHANGING

TEACHER

EDUCATION

INSTITUTIONAL CONSIDERATIONS IN INITIATING CHANGE IN TEACHER EDUCATION

5

HENRIETTA L. BARNES

Overview. In discussing the challenge inherent in transforming knowledge into teacher education programs, this volume has pointed to a number of difficulties and complications that stem from a need to reconceptualize teaching and teacher education. Not only must teacher educators think differently about teaching and what prospective teachers must know and do to ensure that all their pupils learn more content at higher levels than ever before in history, but, we also have to question seriously how prospective teachers acquire such capabilities. Along with constructing new definitions of teacher education knowledge, we have to wonder how programs of initial teacher preparation can contribute to the abilities and propensities that are needed. As we contemplate the latter we must confront old stereotypes about who the teacher educators are and dispel the myth that only those who reside in colleges and departments of education qualify. Whether for good or ill, many educators currently contribute to the conceptions of teaching, learning, and schooling that novices bring to their first teaching assignments. For example, faculties in the arts and sciences, as well as faculties in K-12 schools, are important educators of teachers. As such, members of these groups need to participate broadly in the planning and delivery of teacher education programs. The changes needed are formidable and absolutely necessary.

■ ■ ■ ■ ■

But bringing about such changes suggests new meaning for the concept of challenge. According to Webster, common use of this word refers to disputes, confrontations, or defiance. Thus, to challenge is to call into account or into question, or to invite into competition. And that is exactly what is happening as faculty at institutions attempt to change their programs of teacher education. As bold initiatives are proposed on campus after campus, these ideas are threatening business as usual. These proposals confront fundamental beliefs and attitudes, defy simplistic responses, call for faculty to cross over traditional disciplinary boundaries, and lead to disputes over turf and control. The forces that inhibit change show themselves almost immediately when this happens, and obstacles are often created to either defeat the proposed changes outright or reduce their potency so that any changes that are made do not fundamentally alter basic assumptions or practices. Yet sustained efforts to realize substantial reform of teacher education are critical if the education of teaching professionals is to improve. Consideration of the roots of resistance to change reveals the magnitude of the problems and the reasons why reforms are so slow in coming and so difficult to realize (Cohen, 1988). Recognition of the institutional, faculty, and leadership characteristics that must be present to bring about change suggests promising avenues to pursue and pitfalls to avoid.

Anyone presuming to bring about change within an established institutional context inevitably encounters difficulties that are embedded within the fabric of norms and historical precedents peculiar to that place. The success or failure of efforts to institutionalize innovations rests, in large part, on the ability of individuals providing leadership to modify those institutional features that impede progress toward desired goals. Insights about the institutional constraints discussed in this chapter emerged from a project supported by the Exxon Education Foundation, designed to explore the difficulties and dilemmas of transforming the knowledge base into the curriculum and programs of 11 large, midwestern institutions. The project included faculty, department chairs, and deans from 11 institutions who were attempting to bring about substantial change in their teacher education programs. The project's intent was to identify the sort of difficulties institutions were experiencing and to define the issues and questions that faculty and administrators need to address. In particular, participants explored the interaction between the desired curriculum and the context. Special attention was given to the ways in which the context enables, prevents, inhibits, or limits the integrity of the curriculum. Participants examined these questions from five different perspectives that emerged from both the research literature and from reflection on what was happening in the various institutions. Initially, five screens were used to examine cases of change efforts presented by participants. The five screens focused on:

- organizing the knowledge base for teacher education curricula,

- outlining conceptions of learning to teach,

- defining essential elements of program and structure,

- promoting organizational change, and

- developing leadership.

Case analyses focused on these questions but led to an inevitable consideration of the political and institutional complexities of curriculum reform. It was apparent throughout our discussions that institutional histories, norms, and expectations represent major obstacles to change. In particular, these realities of academic life are apparent with regard to the organization of teacher education programs and in the policies and practices involving faculty work. ■

■

CONSIDERATION ONE: THE ORGANIZATION OF TEACHER EDUCATION

More often than not, proposals to change teacher educa-tion are met with resistance steeped in institutional tradition. In many universities, teacher education is considered to be an all-university responsibility. On a practical level this means that responsibility for different parts of the preparation program is dispersed across different units of the university. This would be a happy circum-stance if there were commitments from all units on the common aims and purposes of programs and a continuing coordination around these goals. In reality, however, it generally means that each unit assumes responsibility for the one piece of the program that is within their domain, without accurate knowledge or understanding of what those responsible for other parts of the program are thinking and doing.

■ ■ ■ ■ ■

Thus, specialized disciplinary study is disconnected from more general study of the disciplines that guide human knowledge and experience. And pedagogy and practice are isolated, often from each other, but also almost completely from other parts of the program. While this characterization is accurate for both secondary and elementary preparation programs, there are still some important distinctions between the two, which pose different problems for teacher education reform.

SECONDARY PREPARATION

On many campuses, secondary teacher candidates major in the fields they are preparing to teach. As majors, they are advised by faculty in those departments that offer the major, and as prospective teachers are subject to all of the college requirements for students pursuing any of the specialty areas offered by that college. Thus, their academic programs are fashioned around perceptions of what well-educated individuals in that field should know about their field, as well as what they, as liberally educated individuals, should know in general. Few would argue with the premise that prospective teachers should have deep understandings of their disciplines and broad knowledge of other areas as well.

The problem arises with the fact that a typical undergraduate degree is normally limited to a maximum number of credit hours. If students are, in fact, going to be liberally educated, it will require most or all of these credit hours to begin a learning process that will, hopefully, continue beyond the undergraduate years. Because the task of providing depth in a specialized field as well as liberal perspectives on other fields is a daunting one in itself, there is little room left for professional study. As a result, education courses are often tolerated as a necessary condition for certification but seen as nonessential for achieving the goals the department has for its majors.

Historically, the number of education courses permitted in programs for prospective secondary teachers has been kept to a minimum. It is not uncommon for secondary students to take one course in educational psychology, one in social-philosophical foundations, one in methods of teaching, and sometimes, depending on state mandates, one in the teaching of content area reading, topped off by one semester of student teaching. Because such configurations are so common and of such long standing across institutions, they must stem historically from some widespread assumptions about teaching. Speculations about what these beliefs might be include the following:

- knowing one's subject is sufficient for being able to teach it;

- novices do not need to understand much about the learners or the context within which they will teach in order to teach subject matter; or

- novices can learn what they need to know about learners and teaching contexts on the job, as students or first year teachers.

There are undoubtedly other viable possibilities. The fact of the matter is, however, that education courses are often seen as service courses to secondary majors in other departments. Thus, the professional preparation component of secondary education programs is frequently given short shrift. As a result, secondary teachers are often criticized for their lack of knowledge about learners and the contexts of teaching. Programs for preparing secondary teachers typically resemble the pattern described above. They have been constructed by allocating credit blocks and responsibility to separate units for specialty area subjects, general education, and professional education coursework. The responsibility for determining the content within each of these blocks is executed by different groups, sometimes without serious consideration of the ends to which that knowledge will be used. Seldom is careful scrutiny given to making the total program more coherent.

On some campuses, however, the departments responsible for preparation in the major field are responsible for all aspects of the program. Motivated by the desire to prepare individuals to teach the subject matters that comprise their fields, departments (English, music, and foreign languages, for example) sometimes provide both the coursework in their disciplines and the pedagogy and practice components of the program as well. Student teaching may or may not be the department's responsibility, and general education studies typically remain outside their purview.

Both of these organizational patterns present problems for teacher education reform. When components of the program are scattered across units of the university, the parts are frequently fragmented from one another. Education courses required for certification are often tolerated as requirements but seldom are conceptually integrated into the preparation programs. While preparation programs tend to be more coherent when departments construct and carry out their own programs of teacher preparation, these programs vary enormously from one department to the other. Teacher candidates in one major field may have a great deal of graduated clinical experience prior to their student teaching, while other candidates from the same university may have little or no such opportunity to learn from and about practice. Since there are few precedents within such programs for collaboration among faculties in the liberal arts and K-12 schools, developing common understandings about what constitutes quality in such programs is cumbersome at best. When secondary programs are located in multiple departments, achieving more uniform quality across programs borders on the impossible. Getting stakeholders to share decision making concerning a curriculum that has historically been their domain represents a major challenge. Thus, the challenges associated with improving the quality of the program are both conceptual and political.

In both situations, getting all parts of a system that has operated separately to function together is complicated. Working collaboratively across units to improve the education of teachers may mean giving up some of the autonomy previously held by separate units. Conceptually, disciplinary faculty may hold disparate views, both within and across departments, about what constitutes understanding of a field. In general, however, faculty agree that one can never know enough about the subject matter one teaches. Thus, the difficulties more often involve differences between college of education faculty and faculty in other departments of the university regarding perceptions of what constitutes essential knowledge for beginning teachers.

Both scenarios described above pertain to arrangements for persons planning to study a discipline and then teach in secondary school. The difficulties mentioned involve questions about the content and control of the curriculum, not whether or not departments should accept such students into their majors. The opportunity for high school teachers to study the subjects they will teach is seen by faculty in disciplinary departments as part of their work. Preparing students to teach subject matter at the elementary level is yet another matter.

ELEMENTARY PREPARATION

In most universities, the responsibility for programs for elementary certification is lodged in schools, departments, or colleges of education. Such programs typically do not require concentrated study in any of the subject matters taught in the lower grades. Thus, prospective elementary teachers take a broad range of courses across different departments of the university. These courses are often introductory in nature and barely skim the surface of the knowledge areas being taught in the elementary school curriculum. Explanations for this circumstance stem from the notion that teachers do not need to know more about a subject than is typically covered in the textbook.

The idea that teachers may need deep understandings of subject matter in order to help young children understand the most basic ideas of a discipline is not prominent among faculty, including many faculty within colleges of education. But the most distressing reason given for not requiring rigorous study of subject matter stems from a fundamental belief that those individuals who choose to teach young children are not capable of in-depth understanding of the disciplines they will teach. The view that prospective elementary teachers cannot succeed within rigorous programs of academic study persists, in part, because admission criteria for elementary education programs have historically been low, and because elementary teacher candidates have frequently ranked among the lowest in many universities on admission tests. In response to widespread criticism of this practice, however, admission standards have been raised significantly in many universities. These institutions now claim that students who wish to seek teacher certification are equal to those entering other fields. In fact, it is not unusual to hear reports that grade point averages of 3.0 and higher are common on many campuses. Despite the fact that these students may have accumulated strong academic records, often in the same courses as their secondary counterparts, this stereotype is well established and interferes with the willingness of disciplinary departments to consider serious proposals to change the content of the teaching majors and minors for prospective elementary teachers.

The fact that disciplinary faculty can seek to include more coursework in the disciplines for students planning to teach at the secondary level, at a time when they are reluctant to include elementary teacher candidates as students within their majors is inherently contradictory, of course. That these stances can be taken simultaneously illustrates another factor involved in teacher education reform; prospective elementary teachers are not the sort of students that disciplinary departments typically seek as majors. This circumstance can be explained on grounds other than those cited above. For one thing, most faculty in disciplinary departments are relatively unfamiliar with the subject matter taught in the elementary classroom. Faculties' own interest in their discipline probably evolved from experiences they had in middle or high school, in or out of school contexts. While they were undoubtedly successful in learning elementary content, they may not have given much, if any, thought to what is or should be taught to young children about their discipline. Faculty study of their own discipline has often reached such an advanced level that it is difficult for them to contemplate which fundamental principles in their fields should be taught at different levels, or how that content might be learned. Another reason is that disciplinary departments are, by and large, primarily interested in preparing persons who will study their disciplines for their own sake, not for any utilitarian purposes. Thus, the most appealing undergraduate student to have as a major is a person who will go on to study at the graduate level. A student who does not expect to pursue advanced study, and even worse, a person who is presumed to be unable to understand the fundamental ideas of a discipline is not perceived to be an ideal student. Such students may be considered by faculty not to be serious students of the discipline and should not use up, so to speak, large amounts of the department's resources. Allowing such students to enroll in upper level courses is problematic since such courses are limited in number and are often taught by the best of the department's faculty.

For elementary teachers to gain access to advanced knowledge in the disciplines that undergird subject matter, all departments on the campus must consider these students to be among the best. In addition, faculty must not only accept the premise that prospective elementary teachers can learn such content, but they must also assume the obligation to provide such knowledge. Although current perceptions will not change automatically when elementary candidates are taught in regular classes with other majors, such attitudes surely will not be altered until these students are given a chance to demonstrate their intellectual capacities.

THE ORGANIZATION OF PROFESSIONAL STUDIES

Just as the different components of a preparation program can be controlled by separate departments, so can the areas of knowledge that comprise the professional studies component itself. More often than not, different departments within a college of education are given responsibility for different requirements in the certification program. Thus, the Educational Psychology department may teach courses on learners and learning, another department may be responsible for courses on school and society or social philosophical foundations, yet another department may offer courses on methods of teaching in the elementary school, and possibly many departments on methods of teaching in secondary schools. And still another department may manage student teaching.

The difficulties of bringing greater coherence to the professional studies program also parallels those associated with the total program. Questions of content and curriculum control must be overcome here, as well as within the larger context of the university. As in the broader university arena, different aspects of educational programs may be developed individually by different units. This practice allows individual features of critical knowledge areas to be addressed more intensively; however, it tends to reinforce the view that knowledge of one area can be understood apart from knowledge of another. The practice of allowing faculty to develop courses apart from consideration of program goals is often supported on the grounds that individual faculty have "academic freedom" rights that should not be constrained. Such an interpretation of academic freedom is, of course, a distortion of the intention of that faculty right. Designed to protect the right of faculty to discuss controversial content, this "freedom" is often construed to mean that only the instructor can determine the content of the courses he or she teaches. In institutions where the latter interpretation prevails, this institutional norm can represent a barrier to collective program planning.

Tensions may also spring from different priorities of different faculty groups and from competition for scarce college resources to support different ends. Or, faculty interests may conflict with college needs. For example, the desire of certain faculty to engage in research may be in competition with the college's need to generate student credit hours. Or, conflicts may reside in faculty being treated differentially. For instance, though courses required for initial and continuing certification often generate a larger number of student credit hours than other courses, teaching such courses may not be seen as the most prestigious work of the college. Thus, faculty who teach teachers may be disproportionately engaged in such work to the exclusion of research activity, while graduate teaching and research may be the domain of a select few. Further, those faculty who work directly in schools with teachers and teacher candidates may be almost totally isolated from interactions from other colleagues on campus. Thus, any opportunity for mutual exchange and growth is circumvented.

Changing these circumstances requires altering the way teacher education is organized within colleges of education. Not only must a college be united by a common purpose and shared goals, it must provide opportunities for faculty to achieve these goals without sacrificing their allegiance to their areas of specialization. Common assumptions about how to achieve those goals must guide the work. Support for the sort of cross disciplinary collaboration that is needed must also be provided. But the professional studies component of teacher education programs will not be improved by addressing organizational questions alone.

THE CONTENT OF PROFESSIONAL STUDIES

Bringing the parts of a program into one unit may or may not facilitate real change in prospective teachers' understandings of teaching. If the professional preparation program does not ensure that students will have the opportunity to examine their entering assumptions and construct grounded understandings of teaching, then the design of the program must also be changed. If the way that the curriculum is enacted does not allow students to develop the capacity to teach a broad range of children within a wide variety of contexts, then the delivery of that program must be altered. If the program does not prepare novices to move away from the image of teaching as telling, learning as accumulating, and knowing as recalling, then both the substance and the nature of learning experiences provided teacher candidates must be examined. And, if the program does not advance broader conceptions of the professional responsibilities and roles of the teacher, the conceptual framework must be altered.

Redesigning the teacher education program requires, above all, that faculty suspend temporarily their own professional and personal interests in order to make tough-minded judgments about the current effectiveness of the program. Wherever deficits in either the content or the teaching of that content are found, they must be corrected. New images of teaching and learning and different conceptions of what constitutes a program must guide such work. In their book, *Profiles of Preservice Teacher Education*, Howey and Zimpher (1989) describe important characteristics of coherent programs. They point to the importance of such features as themes, a conceptual framework, the integration of research and practice in the development of that framework, and articulation between and among different courses and between campus and field experiences as essential for the conceptual integrity of the program. Further, Howey and Zimpher note the importance of faculty collegiality, the presence of a program identity or ethos, and the sense of shared ordeal on the part of both faculty and students as important aspects of coherent programs. Such features are seen as important because they facilitate the development of grounded schemas for guiding teacher judgment and action. Given that teaching is primarily intellectual work, the development of coherent programs of teacher education must be a priority consideration in any redesign attempts.

Howey and Zimpher (1989) point out, however, that curriculum reformers must also address other priorities. In their analysis of the curriculum of the six institutions studied, they note the absence of themes focusing "on the moral and ethical dimensions of what is a highly moral endeavor. . .the dominant emphasis in most institutions remains on the technical and communicative dimensions of teaching" (Howey & Zimpher, 1989, p. 258). For all children to have equitable access to empowering knowledge, the curriculum must address this omission.

Preparation to engage in any sort of professional practice that does not include attention to questions of ethical behavior are, by definition, incomplete. For teachers, however, this curricular omission is significant when it means that content critical to success in teaching itself is omitted from the curriculum. Coursework that highlights issues of diversity and equity represents such an area. Usually referred to as multicultural education, this area includes knowledge of cultures and contexts but goes beyond familiarity with the mores and traditions of different groups to advance the role of teachers as advocates for learners, teachers who are willing to confront institutional constraints that create barriers to learning for all students.

While few will argue about the importance of this goal, faculty may resist attempts to give sufficient time in the curriculum to develop the understandings, propensities, and abilities that are needed to ensure that all youngsters in a variety of contexts will develop the deep understandings they will need of subject matter and other important content. This resistance stems from two sources; one has to do with the numbers game. Given the finite number of courses that can be offered and the differing priorities about what beginning teachers need to know, allocating credits to one area results in reduced attention to another. The other source of resistance comes from the fact that faculty may not be convinced that curricular space given to the study of diversity and equity issues substantially improves the beginning teacher's ability to foster student understanding. A relatively small body of empirical data exists concerning the ways that knowledge of different cultures and contexts inform, appropriately, the judgments that teachers make. Cazden and Mehan (1989) in their chapter in the KBBT volume have summarized the knowledge they believe teachers must have concerning cultural understanding. Until recently, however, little attention has been given to the ways that knowledge of such factors might affect the learning of subject matter. Studies undertaken by Vasquez (1989) and Contreras (1987) are promising and point not only to the contributions that cultural experience can bring to learning but also to the need for teacher knowledge in this area. Yet, studies of how teachers use knowledge about the families and communities in which children live and the school contexts within which they are educated are not well represented in the literature and are largely absent in the KBBT volume.

Similarly, calls for teachers to be better prepared to work within diverse settings abound and are growing (Sleeter & Grant, 1990). Attempts to infuse such perspectives into professional studies courses have been disappointing, however, and make it difficult for teacher educators to argue the benefits for including such study within preparation programs (McDiarmid & Price, 1989; NCRTE, 1988). Thus, it is incumbent on those who understand the importance of such subject matter for teaching to help the educational community define the body of knowledge that is critical; articulate how such knowledge can inform, and not misinform, judgments about children's learning; and create new ways of fostering critical understandings about culture and community within teacher education programs (Dilworth, 1990).

It is also essential that knowledge about culture and community become connected to knowledge about the disciplines that undergird subject matter and the pedagogy for representing the ideas of the discipline to children. Making these connections may help teachers interpret the meanings children are constructing about a subject area and provide productive avenues to explore in their attempts to engender passion for a discipline. Knowing about the contributions members of diverse cultures have made to law, literature, and mathematics, for example, may be the hook that engenders a learner's enthusiasm for certain areas of study. In the movie *Stand and Deliver*, Jaime Escalante used such knowledge to capture the attention and enthusiasm of his students for math when he told them, "Your people discovered zero. It is in your blood." Such connections mean a great deal to children who feel like outsiders. Furthermore, all of these knowledge areas must be tied to practice. Knowledge is not simply transferred from one context to another, it must be transformed in light of essential qualities of the new situation.

If teachers are to use important knowledge in their daily teaching, they must be able to draw on the knowledge frameworks they have constructed through their own study, experiences, and reflections about practice as they learn to teach. Helping prospective teachers construct cognitive frameworks that represent networked understandings is the substance of professional study. While this is intellectual work, it must be grounded in experiences within which the teaching of a subject is done with diverse learners in multiple settings. Such experiences are iterative and require opportunities for reflection on the similarities and differences in conditions as well as approaches to pedagogy undertaken.

Preparing beginning teachers who have the dispositions and capacities to engage in professional judgment, action, and reflection will require greater, not less, space in the initial teacher education program. This conception of the sort of knowledge and experiences prospective teachers need in order to begin to teach changes the purposes of initial preparation significantly. No longer is it possible to offer theoretical knowledge divorced from a consideration of its uses. Nor is it acceptable to assume that by passing courses, teacher candidates have acquired the understandings, dispositions, and abilities they will need for professional practice.

The view that disciplinary knowledge can be taught separately from pedagogy and that both of these can be learned apart from knowledge about culture, community, and practice prevails despite efforts to counter this perspective through deliberation and written documents. This point of view is significant because it influences the number of professional study credits within a program that the university community, and the broader public sector, are willing to support. But, the possibility that the resistance is not conceptual only must also be considered. By not accepting the conceptual argument grounded in a new definition of teacher education, faculty both within and outside the college of education protect themselves from change. It is then possible for faculty and whole departments to choose not to change on the grounds that they are unconvinced that teachers will be better prepared by the type of program described.

CONSIDERATION TWO: CHANGING THE NORMS FOR FACULTY WORK

Reluctance to change is typically very personal since faculty work and futures are inextricably linked with the norms of the institutions within which they work. Although often cast as conceptual, political, or fiscal reservations, questions are strongly motivated by concerns that grow out of fear that new ways of doing teacher education will seriously affect how faculty work is construed. At every level of discussion concerning reform, these fears are likely to surface. The same questions are addressed, the same anxieties are expressed, and the same kinds of resistance are articulated. Often seen as turf protection or power struggles over control of the curriculum, these questions have to do with the worry that faculty will find no place for their expertise within the new scheme of things, or that they will not be as successful at the new work that is envisioned, or that the new work will not be perceived as valuable by their professional colleagues at other universities, or that it will not be sufficiently accepted by their peers in other departments at their current university. These worries are very real and sensible, given the organization of universities and the reward systems typically used. Attempts to reform curriculum inevitably threaten traditional norms for how one does one's work and how that work will be recognized. Thus, institutions that are serious about a reform agenda must also be serious about changing the norms of their own institutions to support that agenda.

EXPECTATIONS FOR FACULTY WORK

Among the norms that must be changed, top priority must be given to creating new expectations for faculty work. What is needed is cross-disciplinary collaboration that cuts across traditional departmental boundaries and extends to work in K-12 settings. Such work is intensive and time consuming, to say the least, but exciting and growth producing for those who do it. Such work is interactive and demanding. It requires coordination, communication, willingness to live with ambiguity, and acceptance of human error. To be productive, however, such work must be built on shared understanding of desirable goals and promising ways of pursuing these purposes. Developing these understandings requires extended opportunity to think and work together over time.

Once conceptualized, however, the curriculum must be enacted by faculty. In order for them to make the commitments and investments that may be needed, these individuals must be able to wrap their own specialized interests around the larger, collective goals being addressed. They must see ways to pursue the research agenda they have carved out for themselves within the context of the program itself. Thus, faculty might be teaching preservice students and working with experienced teachers in a variety of settings around particular instructional issues and, simultaneously, studying questions that are relevant to their own line of inquiry. Integrating faculty work so that teaching, research, and service are closely connected inevitably has implications for where faculty will do their work.

Increasingly, faculty work will need to be carried out in K-12 classrooms, schools, and communities. The need to link theoretical perspectives on teaching with actual teaching requires that those who teach teachers remain connected to classrooms. In addition, however, faculty will need to work closely with experienced teachers who can provide thoughtful mentoring of novices. Such involvement may lead these educators to combine their talents to address instructional and schooling dilemmas together. Such work may take a variety of forms. At times university faculty may teach children on a regular basis in order to study particular instructional problems. This work might provide a laboratory for classroom teachers, who might observe students or collect other data that might be analyzed by a team of university and school colleagues studying the issues together. At other times, more traditional forms of inquiry, demonstration teaching, observations, and discussions might be ongoing. In still other situations, university and school faculty might be working with community leaders and parents to improve conditions or gain parental support for educational programs of the school.

Similarly, the nature of collaborative inquiry might need to be defined and supported in various ways. The traditional separation of research on teaching and teacher education from teaching practice, both in the K-12 sector and on campus, is a major obstacle to change. The study of teaching is a powerful vehicle for improving one's teaching practice. For those who teach teachers it is an important opportunity to gain understanding about both the content one is teaching and the meaning different representations of the content may have for learners. Conversely, it is essential that those who study teaching engage in teaching students who will use the insights from such research in their classroom interactions with learners. Through such instruction, researchers can both validate and extend their own understandings of the subtle ways that different contexts can alter the usefulness of research findings for informing practice.

Over the past two decades, the traditional norms for doing research have changed. Classroom research has now become commonplace, and research on one's own practice is emerging as a useful paradigm (Lampert & Clark, 1990). Professional debates now focusing on the usefulness for practice of research knowledge call attention to the need for educators to broaden their conceptions of the forms of research activity that must be developed. Building on notions of collaborative inquiry (Richardson, 1990), new forms of inquiry are evolving from early collaborations between teachers and researchers during the '70s and '80s. For example, teacher collaborators were included on all projects of the Institute for Research on Teaching (Porter, 1986) and in Ward and Tikunuff's (1977) studies of interactive teaching studies. Similarly, projects supported through Teacher Corps (Barnes & Putnam, 1981; Lanier, 1983) demonstrated the value of combining developmental efforts with serious study of both the processes used and outcomes resulting from collaborative work. While traditional forms of inquiry may be used in collaborative inquiry, this approach is characterized by the fact that both development of new teaching practice and systematic inquiry are combined into a form of educational inquiry that is particularly suited for the study of teaching.

In contrast to traditional forms of research, in which persons who may be unfamiliar with the context sometimes study an activity that may be foreign to them, the researchers in collaborative inquiry understand the activity and the context in which the activity is taking place. Such research and development efforts engage university and classroom teachers in all phases of the activity and may involve university faculty teaching in K-12 classrooms. Unlike more conventional forms of research, collaborative inquiry does not seek findings from relatively short-term study of classroom episodes. Rather, collaborative inquiry attempts to generate insights that can be contemplated by the participants themselves and elaborated for successive trials in the same and other settings by participants studying a particular teaching problem. The definition of the problem that may be tied to particular contexts and learners is the continuing subject of inquiry, in the same way that various responses to different definitions of the problem are explored through continuing study. Initial insights from first attempts are just that—tentative conclusions drawn from first trial attempts. The insights that follow may serve to deepen and strengthen original findings or suggest the limitations of those findings. The promise of this form of inquiry for improving both teaching and teacher education is encouraging. However, norms within most colleges of education do not support such faculty work. Instead of fostering sustained, collaborative study, current norms for allocating faculty time and rewarding faculty work tend to encourage short-term projects and studies that can reach fruition quickly. Changing these norms is critical if research and practice are to become better integrated.

CHANGING FACULTY LOAD ASSIGNMENTS

For new forms of faculty work to be envisioned by faculty, they must see that the work is both possible and valuable. Work of the sort described above is more likely to occur when faculty loads are reasonable and flexible. If norms for allocating faculty teaching loads are rigid, however, only the most visionary faculty will be able to imagine how to create opportunities to do serious work in schools. Similarly, if heavy teaching loads are the norm, only the most dedicated will find ways to do sustained work in schools. Teaching four courses a semester on campus to large groups of students does not allow teacher educators to develop new ways to advance teacher understandings or to reflect on their effectiveness as teacher educators.

Once faculty have conceptualized a new curriculum and made commitments to work in K-12 classrooms and schools, structures for allocating load time should be examined and modified, as necessary, to make them responsive to the nature of faculty work envisioned, and new models for teaching students may need to be developed. For example, instead of being assigned to teach one course to 30 students for one semester, faculty might be assigned to form a study group of 15 students to focus on a particular issue or content area over time. If time for deliberation among university and school colleagues is needed, such discussions must be seen as an important part of the faculty member's work. Just as teachers need time for intellectual dialogue and reflection about their work, teacher educators must have time to plan collaboratively and reflect with colleagues about their students' learning. Load time must allocate time for this work as well.

EVALUATING FACULTY WORK

Changing the nature of faculty work may require substantial changes in the ways that faculty productivity is defined and rewarded. Faculty must feel that their efforts are not only valuable for themselves and their immediate students, but they must feel that it is supported and recognized by their peers in the department, college, and the university at large. Traditionally, faculty productivity is judged on the quality and number of research articles generated. Developmental work of the sort described above is generally referred to as service activity. Rewards for good work in this arena are typically not commensurate with those granted good research.

If faculty work is to become better integrated across areas of teaching research and development or service, these activities must be equally valued for their potential to advance professional understandings. Policies for evaluating the scholarly productivity of faculty must explicitly recognize the importance of each of these forms of faculty work. In forming such policies, it should not matter whether faculty are teaching, doing systematic research, or are engaged in sustained school improvement activities. What should matter is the quality of scholarship that the faculty member is bringing to that activity. To be of value, school improvement efforts and teaching itself should be both products of strong scholarship and opportunities for scholarly work. Thus, policies for evaluating faculty scholarship should indicate the forms of evidence that can be put forward for peer review of such scholarship. Whether that scholarship is demonstrated through activity that is primarily teaching, or research, or service is of less consequence than are questions concerning the nature of the evidence one can put forward for review.

In addition to establishing policies that recognize scholarly work in all areas of faculty work, attention must also be given to ways to recognize differences in the complexity, difficulty, and level of responsibility involved in the work that faculty do. As indicated earlier, collaborative development and inquiry are complicated and difficult. Coordinating coherent programs of teacher education places greater responsibility on program leaders than does more conventional approaches to teacher education. Maintaining the conceptual integrity of thematic programs demands that time be devoted to coordinating the work of several university and school faculty across multiple dimensions over time. Studying and evaluating programmatic work is multilayered and complex. Faculty who do this sensitive and labor-intensive work well are essential to the success of these programs. Unless evaluation systems are examined for their ability to reward such work, it is unlikely that coherent programs of teacher education can be sustained.

■

CONSIDERATION THREE:
LEADERSHIP FOR CHANGE

As a form of social change, teacher education reform cannot be accomplished solely through the formal leadership of the dean or the department chair. Leadership is required at all levels and from all participants. Yet formal leaders can and do make a tremendous difference in initiating reforms and in creating the conditions for institutionalizing those reforms.

Formal leaders are both advantaged and constrained by their roles. For example, deans and department chairs can define, strengthen, and articulate the enduring values and distinctive qualities of the institution. They can set an agenda, establish priorities, and reconcile competing interests. In addition, they can stimulate, empower, and support faculty who demonstrate potential as conceptual leaders and organizational change agents. To support the efforts of these informal leaders, formal leaders can obtain and allocate resources, provide incentives, distribute rewards, and buffer external forces and internal strains. Since the total system that exists has high inertia, anything that requires a coordinated effort is unlikely to be started or maintained. Formal leaders can sustain the effort by giving time and energy to the decision-making process. They can be persistent in studying the problem, providing information, focusing on substantive issues, and facilitating participation from the opposition. If the presence of competing interests are stalling the effort, formal leaders can deflect attention away from the primary reform effort by supporting multiple faculty activities.

While they may try to legislate change and control the process of change itself, formal leaders are dependent on faculty for the success of the reform effort. For the most part, deans and department chairs can effect change —when their faculty feel confident and take initiative. When faculty feel proud of

■   ■   ■   ■   ■

their institutions and want their leaders to succeed, the task is further facilitated. In addition, however, faculty must be tolerant of ambiguity, willing to take risks, and capable of altering their roles and functions. To be successful, deans and department chairs must have the capacity to stimulate faculty's interest so that it catches fire and to work toward successive approximations of their imagined ideal. Of primary importance is the ability of the formal leader to allow informal faculty leadership to emerge and evolve responsibly. Disparate faculty views and priorities must be acknowledged and accommodated within a common agenda. Allowing diverse approaches to accomplish a shared agenda will strengthen the likelihood that faculty can move forward together.

The presence of strong leadership among both faculty and administrators is, of course, the ideal. Working in concert, new visions of curriculum can be forged, and institutional structures to support these images can be created. Neither faculty nor administrators can accomplish the task alone. This is true partly because each group controls different domains of influence. That is, faculty have authority over the content of the curriculum, while administrators have responsibility for allocating resources to support the approved curriculum. But these distinctions extend also to consideration of ways that availability of resources can influence the substance and character of the curriculum itself. The ability to envision new images of teaching and teacher education depends partly on the ability to imagine new ways to use the resources of faculty time and talent to achieve the multiple purposes of the institution. Together, formal and informal college leaders can construct bold proposals.

Sustained, systematic attention to the reform agenda is necessary if it is to succeed. Pervasive, congruent, formal, and informal communication networks must be established and maintained over extended periods of time. Serious connections between research and practice must be constructed and sustained if the system is to be self-renewing and authentic.

■

CONSIDERATION FOUR: ALTERNATIVE APPROACHES TO CHANGE

Depending on the institutional history, norms, and expectations for faculty work that prevail within a given college or university, different approaches to change may be appropriate. If a program has remained unchanged for some time, the most efficacious means of initiating change may be through support of one or more experimental efforts. Involvement in such programs will allow interested faculty to test the desirability and the feasibility of a new approach without the burden of having to convince others on the basis of argument alone. In this case, the initial work may move forward relatively unimpeded. However, unless faculty sustain their commitment to bring others into the enterprise, to keep the broader community informed about their work, and to use their efforts as a springboard for later consideration of more comprehensive change, the experimental program will likely remain outside the mainstream offerings of the college or university.

In other cases, where pilot programs have already been tried, faculty may wish to seek broad support for a revised curriculum. Depending on the context, proposals for change may be met with some of the conceptual and political problems described above. Counter proposals may be made, and concessions may be necessary to gain support for a new curriculum.The danger here is that some concessions may compromise the integrity of the reform agenda itself. Thus, it is critical that faculty be clear about what changes will move the agenda forward and what will not.

In any event, proposals for serious reform of teacher preparation require that new possibilities be envisioned and adopted. When responsibility for different parts of the program are dispersed among several academic units, the likelihood that all of these units will coalesce around a common agenda is small. In such situations, it makes sense either to mount serious efforts to develop shared understandings or to consider ways to circumvent these units.

One way to accomplish the first goal is through sustained dialogue across all stakeholders. This approach, which was used by one of the insti-

■ ■ ■ ■ ■

tutions in Michigan State University's Exxon project, is described later in this volume. The danger inherent in this approach is that political considerations may dominate the discussion and may interfere with the faculty's ability to focus on the conceptual issues involved in curriculum development.

Another way to bring coherence to the curriculum is to place responsibility for the total program within a center that exists outside the usual departmental structure of the university. While this is an appealing alternative, there is a danger that this special unit will not have sufficient authority to garner the faculty expertise and financial resources needed to effect and institutionalize the curriculum that is created.

Regardless of the approach that is adopted, efforts to bring about change must be undertaken with the understanding that change is usually incremental. Whether change is attempted through efforts to alter the content of one course, or one component of a program, or by reconceptualizing a total program, there is always the hazard that the initial effort will become an end in itself. It is very difficult to sustain efforts to make systemic curriculum changes. Changing smaller parts of the total system is easier to manage, and more likely to be experienced as meaningful by faculty. Improvements that are created through these efforts are usually satisfying for those who have developed ownership for this work, while ways to improve within the new framework are initially ambiguous and challenging. Unless the goal of more comprehensive, systemic change is kept visible, therefore, changes will remain local and may not contribute to an ongoing process of curriculum renewal.

Given the nature of incremental change and the need for simultaneous attention to multiple factors, educational change of any consequence must be comprehensive and long term. Sustained efforts are needed. This process might be seen as one of institutionalized reform and represents a new norm for many institutions. It includes conceptualizing, experimenting with, and adopting those features of the reform that show promise of advancing the capacities of beginning professional teachers. Thus, a program is never totally fixed but is always in a state of ongoing development and self-renewal. Integral to this concept, of course, is the serious study and evaluation of such programs.

Conceiving of reform in this way illustrates the long-term nature of this enterprise. In his discussion of factors that inhibit educational reform, Cohen (1988) contends that most people underestimate the complexities, the barriers, and the time frame that is needed to achieve change of the magnitude appointed. Those who understand the complexity, difficulty, and comprehensive quality of the work, and have the courage to do it, must be supported by the institutions within which they work. Changing those institutional characteristics that constrain serious reforms should be given our highest priority.

■

REFERENCES

Barnes, H., & Putnam, J. (1981, February). *Professional development through reciprocity and reflection.* Paper presented at the annual meeting of the American Association of Colleges for Teacher Education, Detroit, MI.

Cazden, C. B., & Mehan, H. (1989). Principles from sociology and anthropology: Context, code, classroom, and culture. In M.C. Reynolds (Ed.), *Knowledge base for the beginning teacher* (pp. 47-58). Oxford, England: Pergamon.

Cohen, D. (1988). Teaching practice: *Plus ca change. . .* In P.W. Jackson (Ed.), *Contributing to educational change: Perspectives on research and practice* (pp. 27-84). Berkeley, CA: McCutcheon.

Contreras, A. (1987). *Constructing subject matter in high school physics: An ethnographic study of three experienced physics teachers.* Unpublished doctoral dissertation, Michigan State University, East Lansing, MI.

Dilworth, M. E. (1990). *Reading between the lines: Teachers and their racial/ ethnic cultures.* Washington, DC: ERIC Clearinghouse on Teacher Education.

Howey, K. R., & Zimpher, N.L. (1989). *Profiles of preservice teacher education: Inquiry into the nature of programs.* Albany: State University of New York Press.

Lampert, M., & Clark, C. M. (1990). Expert knowledge and expert thinking in teaching: A response to Floden and Klinzing. *Educational Researcher, 19*(4), 21-23.

Lanier, J. (1983). *Tensions in teaching teachers the skills of pedagogy.* Eighty-second yearbook of the National Society for Study of Education.

McDiarmid, G., & Price, J. (1989). *Prospective teachers' view of diverse learners: A study of participants in the ABCD Project* (Research Report No. 90-6). East Lansing: Michigan State University, National Center for Research on Teacher Education.

■ ■ ■ ■ ■

National Center for Research on Teacher Education. (1988). *Dialogues in teacher education* (Issue Paper 88-4). East Lansing: Michigan State University, National Center for Research on Teacher Education.

Porter, A. C. (1986). *Collaborating with teachers on research: Pioneering efforts at the Institute for Research on Teaching* (Occasional Paper No. 105). East Lansing: Michigan State University, Institute for Research on Teaching.

Richardson, V. (1990). Significant and worthwhile change in teaching practice. *Educational Researcher, 19*(7), 10-18.

Sleeter, C. E., & Grant, C. A. (1990). *Turning on learning: Five approaches for multicultural teaching plans for race, class, gender, and disability.* Columbus, OH: Merrill Publishers.

Vasquez, O. (1989). *Connecting oral language strategies to literacy: An ethnographic study among four Mexican immigrant families.* Unpublished doctoral dissertation, Stanford University, Stanford, CA.

Ward, B. A., & Tikunuff, W. J. (1977). *Context: Some important considerations for research on teaching* (Report No. A77-4). CA: Far West Laboratory for Education Research and Development.

CASE ONE:
A COLLABORATIVE
STRUCTURE
FOR INSTITUTIONAL
CHANGE
IN TEACHER EDUCATION

6

SUZANNE H. PASCH

MARLEEN C. PUGACH

RICHARD G. FOX

Overview. Strategies for reform can take many different forms, but central to all of them must be collaboration: within professional units that prepare teachers, across teacher education and liberal arts, and between teacher education and the public schools. In this chapter, a collaborative structure for changing the practice of teacher education is described that functions as a unifying umbrella for all aspects of reform. The Center for Teacher Education at the University of Wisconsin-Milwaukee is an experiment in creating an alternative organizational structure that serves as a continuous catalyst for collaborative efforts in teacher education redesign. As a new form of administrative unit, the Center promotes the value of collaboration as the framework within which faculty and practitioners engage in the hard work of programmatic change. ■

In May 1990, the faculty of the School of Education at the University of Wisconsin-Milwaukee (UWM) voted unanimously, and with almost no discussion, to endorse the continuation of the Center for Teacher Education as a permanent unit of the School. Four years earlier, also by vote but following lengthy, impassioned discussion, the faculty established this experimental unit, charged it with reforming teacher education, and then set a sunset clause of three years to revisit it to determine whether the Center should be permitted to continue. The original vote represented a compromise following two years of self-study, and the realization that, at that time, the faculty would neither agree to form a department of teacher education, nor to establish a unit over which it had no continuing control. This turned out to be a serendipitous event. The unwieldy unit born, patted on the bottom, and sent out to survive with an ax over its head, provided precisely the structure that permitted the recent vote, a vote which recognized and affirmed the collaborative, creative work conducted through this interdisciplinary Center that is simultaneously home base to none and home to all.

This chapter focuses on the UWM Center for Teacher Education as a case study in reform. As we move from translating the broad, inspirational goals of the national teacher education agenda to reportable programmatic results, we need to pause and consider the role that structure and process play in our work. The chapter discusses the Center for Teacher Education as a case that highlights those factors. First, we provide an overview of the history, mission, and organization of the Center for Teacher Education and then describe its progress to date. Then, we explore the role of structure in developing a shared vision and enabling institutional reform and discuss the nature of collaborative process as the strategy for accomplishing such change. In this case, the Center for Teacher Education provides an organizational structure that facilitates institutional change by mandating collaborative interaction; the emphasis in the chapter is on describing that structure and specifying the nature of the resultant collaboration. Critical process variables that we have stumbled onto, foreseen, and grappled with, as part of the reform process, are presented and analyzed in sufficient detail to permit some possible generalities to other sites. Observations and recommendations about this attempt to accomplish meaningful change in teacher education within an existing institution and through the application of a collaborative structure complete the chapter.

■

DESCRIPTION OF THE CENTER FOR TEACHER EDUCATION

HISTORY

The effort to reform teacher education programs at UWM began in 1984-85 with a study of the existing situation. A 13-member Task Force on Teacher Education was sponsored by the newly arrived dean and charged with reviewing the current program and developing a plan to guide and initiate reforms. In its final report (UWM School of Education, 1986), the task force noted several strengths of the existing program, but emphasized those areas needing improvement. Like most other traditional programs, the inadequacies cited included the following:

- lack of a coherent, well-sequenced teacher education curriculum;

- no clear connection between the teacher education curriculum and the schools where students gain their field experiences;

- few opportunities to monitor the progress of students through the program;

- lack of adequate preparation in subject areas in some programs; and

- inability to attract and retain minority students in teacher education.

If meaningful change in teacher education programs was to occur, however, UWM needed first to reform its own institutional arrangements to facilitate change and to enable any changes that occurred to remain in place. As is true at many universities, the traditional organization of teacher education at UWM placed the main responsibility with departments for delivering course content and for sequencing course offerings. While this arrangement was convenient for making some decisions, it made it nearly impossible for the faculty to offer a coordinated program, to monitor the program as a whole, to identify problems that existed across department lines, and to institute change in an interdisciplinary manner. In the year following the task force's analysis, a subsequent working group developed a proposal to address these problems. It leaned toward the establishment

■   ■   ■   ■   ■   ■

of a Department of Teacher Education but, faced with political realities inside the school, recommended instead the establishment of a Center for Teacher Education. Thus, the Center for Teacher Education was a compromise based on concerns that a Department of Teacher Education would either draw resources and personnel away from other programs or would fail to develop sufficient faculty support to survive.

Even as a compromise measure, however, establishing the Center for Teacher Education was not accomplished easily. Objections raised to this change included concerns that establishing a separate unit to oversee and recommend changes in teacher education would violate departmental and individual faculty rights, and further, that the Center would be an elitist unit in which faculty would receive reduced teaching loads and other special favors and would have few incentives to work with other colleagues. In an institution that historically prides itself on its shared governance system, these were not trivial arguments. In verbal debate, responses were raised to counter the objections by the Center's supporters. This debate is chronicled in a paper describing the creation of the Center (Schug, Pugach, & Pasch, 1988). In fact, both contemporaneously and in retrospect, none of us knew exactly what was going to happen with the creation of a Center, but some of us wanted to be given the chance to find out.

MISSION AND ORGANIZATION OF THE CENTER

In fall 1986, the faculty of the School of Education voted to establish the Center for Teacher Education. Representation on the Center included faculty from all teacher certification programs and from the foundations departments in the School of Education. Specifically, the 12 Center faculty consisted of one representative each from early childhood education, elementary education, physical education, and secondary education; two representatives from exceptional education; one representative each from cultural foundations and educational psychology; and four at-large faculty representatives, approved by their departments and by the remaining Center faculty. An elementary school principal and a high school teacher were also members of the Center for Teacher Education. This group of 14 people was given responsibility to:

- develop, implement, and evaluate integrated, innovative, and interdisciplinary teacher education programs;

- coordinate and monitor the content of programs leading to teacher certification;

- establish collaborative relationships with area schools to develop effective learning settings for children and youth, prospective teachers, and classroom teachers;

- coordinate the recruitment of qualified students for teacher education programs, giving special attention to recruitment and retention of minority students;

- control entrance to and movement through teacher education programs by recommending entry requirements and specifying admission, advising, and advancement procedures; and

- conduct research on teacher education, teaching, learning, and other factors related to schools and schooling.

This broad agenda was viewed as a fundamental change in the way teacher education was conducted because it charged an identifiable interdisciplinary group with monitoring and improving the diverse elements of UWM teacher education programs. The members of the Center for Teacher Education began meeting in January 1987. An acting director was selected from within the membership and given a term of one and a half years; a subcommittee structure was developed to facilitate the Center's work; and a weekly meeting time was scheduled to work on the evolving agenda.

Not surprisingly, the earliest meetings focused on procedure but quickly moved to substantive issues. In the first few months, participants focused on issues that, in their opinion, filled immediate gaps and needs in the preservice program. Some of these were operational issues that many considered essential to improve professional relationships both within the School of Education and the education community on which UWM relied for clinical sites. Thus, from January to May the group established regular stipends for cooperating teachers; began the effort to centralize field placements (which involved creating a position and lobbying for that position); and identified an evaluator, since by enabling legislation the Center had a three-year sunset provision. Looking to the future, the group also began to draft, in a joint committee with representatives from the Milwaukee Public Schools, a proposal for developing professional development schools in Milwaukee. Participants developed a new course to replace the introductory field experience/colloquium and

planned its gradual implementation. Then the group established more formal relationships with colleagues in the liberal arts and in preservice programs in art and
music education. The Center became involved in national activities related to
teacher education, for example, The Holmes Group. And, perhaps most significantly, it made a commitment that new programs and partnerships would focus on
preparing urban educators. While UWM has always been an urban institution with
an urban mission, that mission has not always been made explicit in the School of
Education or in the university as a whole. Previously, in the School of Education,
for example, many programs with a strong urban focus were limited to small groups
or implemented on an experimental basis. Now an urban focus was adopted for the
whole teacher education program.

PROGRESS

The three-part mission to restructure teacher education
programs, establish effective partnerships with urban schools, and conduct and disseminate research on the processes of change in which UWM participates continues to drive the continually evolving work of the Center. In each of these areas, significant progress has been made. Perhaps as important, though, over time the Center has become a focal point for change. Ideas and outcomes emanate from the Center outward, and ideas developed outside are also brought to the Center for further
consideration and possible adoption. The Center coordinates and synthesizes work
across the School of Education, the university, and in the community. Teacher education has begun to gain the respect of others, and a spirit of reform in areas beyond teacher education appears also to be encouraged by the Center's presence
and example.

A central part of the reform effort involves program development to enhance the quality of prospective teachers graduating from UWM.
Principles guiding program reform efforts, descriptions of program components,
and a timeline for implementation of programmatic changes were all articulated
during the first two years of Center operation. The integrated, thematic program
that developed is designed to prepare effective, beginning urban teachers. Many of
the changes focus on students enrolled in the undergraduate elementary certification program, since, as the largest program, that was the initial focus of the Center.
However, further work is proceeding that will extend the themes and components

just described to the early childhood, secondary, and special education areas; a committee is exploring and recommending changes in postbaccalaureate work consistent with the principles and themes articulated; approval has gone forward for an internship program for minority paraprofessionals and teacher aides working in the Milwaukee Public Schools, and exploratory work continues on extending urban teaching preparation to candidates from other University of Wisconsin System campuses. The work of the Center for Teacher Education in the program area is thus not limited to undergraduate teacher preparation but, rather, provides an umbrella structure for innovation in all aspects of teacher education. In 1988, a permanent director was selected from within the Center membership; in 1989, the Center was designated as a University of Wisconsin System Center of Excellence, one of seven such centers on the UWM campus and the only one in the state devoted to teacher education.

PROGRAM

The philosophy of UWM teacher education programs is to prepare prospective teachers who can deal effectively and reflectively with current realities and conditions of work and who can also play a major role in shaping the future of a more empowered profession. Prospective UWM teachers participate in sequential academic and field-based experiences based on principles of research and sound professional practice. Teacher education students move through three differentiated levels of preparation or blocks and participate in cohort groups that serve to integrate and synthesize program components. Faculty work together and with colleagues from the public schools to deliver the program. Among the accomplishments of the Center to date are:

- an admissions and selections procedure that parallels blocks of coursework and provides for continual monitoring of student progress;

- an initial academic and clinical experience that introduces students to the professional program and emphasizes multicultural education and classroom and school observation;

- a coordinated sequence of work that focuses on psychological and cultural foundations, general and content-specific instructional methods, three models of instruction, and a culminating clinical experience and seminar;

- a thematic approach with four strands of emphasis—urban teaching, developing learners, instruction, and professionalism—that binds the program together and permits students in cohort groups to examine and reexamine concepts integral to the development of an effective entry-level urban educator;

- cohort activities that include reflective journals, case studies, and reading logs, as well as activities that emphasize ongoing self-evaluation, reflective decision-making, integration of academic and clinical experiences, and collaborative interaction as essential to effective teaching;

- integration of liberal studies into pedagogical studies to reinforce the notion that an educated person is at the core of an effective teacher;

- a beginning teacher network, a support group for graduates, plans to extend induction activities through the development of a cooperative mentoring program with Milwaukee Public Schools and the Wisconsin Department of Public Instruction; and

- an extensive set of activities designed to increase recruitment and retention of minority teachers. For instance, the Center has administered a grant that distributes scholarships, hired a staff member to enhance student support, and established a connection with the Milwaukee Area Technical College that brings minority student graduates of their two-year Cooperative Urban Teacher Education Program to UWM for their preservice preparation.

PROFESSIONAL DEVELOPMENT SCHOOLS

The Center's mission includes the improvement of professional practice and, in that context, the designation of professional development schools was an essential step in making the Center's goals operational. In January 1988, two elementary schools, one middle school, and one high school in the Milwaukee Public Schools (MPS) system were designated as MPS/UWM professional development schools (PDS). They are all urban schools with their attendant problems and opportunities. A member of the Center for Teacher Education faculty serves as a liaison for each school. Center faculty worked collaboratively with representatives of the Milwaukee Public Schools to outline the nature and intent of the professional development school concept and to specify criteria to consider in site selection. A selection committee consisting of representatives from the school district and the Center for Teacher Education faculty promoted the concept of professional development schools and selected initial sites. Principals submitted applications to the district. If schools met initial criteria, the selection team visited the school and met with the faculty. To be considered, schools had to possess the following characteristics:

- a diverse student population;
- two or three classes per grade level;
- typical curriculum in a nonspecialty school;
- a range of instructional services including art, music, and physical education;
- exceptional education classes in high incidence categories; and
- access to public transportation.

In addition the staff as a group had to be willing to become involved extensively in preservice education and curricular innovation, maintain an open door policy with all classrooms available for observation, and agree to participate over a three- to five-year period. During school visits, faculty members at potential sites were given opportunities to discuss the concept; no school was placed on the final list of potential sites until the school staff had agreed to apply for consideration. Final decisions were jointly reached and announced by the coordinating committee; the degree of support expressed by the teaching staff was a strong factor in the final decision.

The schools eventually designated as MPS/UWM professional development schools posed particular challenges for the concept of partnership in teacher education and staff development. The two elementary schools, located in Milwaukee's central city, have an almost entirely black student population from low socioeconomic backgrounds in one school, and a mixed black and Hispanic poor student body in the other. At both schools, only small numbers of preservice teachers had previously spent time in the student teaching phase of their programs.

Similarly, the middle school is located in the inner city, has an almost entirely black and low income population, and has a record of low performance on standardized measures of student achievement. Moreover, that school suffers the highest turnover rate for teachers and one of the highest transiency rates for students in the city. The high school has a neighborhood attendance population that is largely black and Hispanic and a citywide magnet component of students who attend because of its designation as a university preparation high school. UWM students have for many years spent time at this high school, and a relationship between the university and the school was firmly established prior to the initiation of professional development schools. However, that contact had been largely limited to the university preparation program.

To summarize, in this case professional development schools have been conceptualized as a partnership designed to address simultaneously issues of teacher preparation, staff development, and school restructuring. The four professional development schools are not "model" schools. With the exception of the high school, the schools with which UWM is working had not engaged in schoolwide curricular change prior to this partnership. The Center's commitment was to involve preservice students in the process of change and to ensure school development as an integral part of their preparation. The intent is that preservice students will see and value professional development and have the opportunity to participate in the process of changing schools as basic parts of their conception of teaching. Over time, the Center for Teacher Education would like the professional development schools to become the centers of inquiry recently described in *Tomorrow's Schools* (The Holmes Group, 1990) and models for addressing the problems of urban schools. Pasch and Pugach (1990) describe events that led to the initial positive outcomes, the interactions experienced to date, and issues that have been raised as a result of the early experiences with professional development schools. A discussion of the issues in collaboration that have developed as a result of these partnerships is presented in subsequent sections of this chapter.

PARTICIPATING IN A COMPREHENSIVE CHANGE PROCESS

Unlike many program-specific reform efforts, the effort assumed by the Center for Teacher Education is an all-encompassing one that affects every teacher education student and faculty member in the School of Education. The Center is a stimulus for ongoing change, and its approach is one that builds tensions designed to encourage creativity and avoid complacency. While sharing details about the operation of the Center and its accomplishments is important as context, it is perhaps most important to share the Center's ethos and how it has affected the lives of those who are Center members and the general atmosphere in the School of Education since its inception. Thus, we move next to describing the process that led to these results, and the effects on faculty lives and institutional character that the establishment of the Center has influenced.

What we share in the remainder of this chapter is really a story of what can happen when faculty members choose to allow the common goal of ongoing improvement of teacher education in the broadest sense to drive their actions and thoughts. In the case of the Center, the goal crosses departmental lines and allegiances and involves practice and the study of practice in teacher education. While initial agreement to serve on the Center might have seemed like an a priori commitment to a common goal regarding teacher education—a goal larger than the needs of individual departments—we have learned that the recognition of that commonality is clearly a developmental process and one not yet completed. Of particular importance in that developmental process is the role of structure and collaborative interaction in facilitating the work of teacher education reform.

■

USING STRUCTURE TO FACILITATE INSTITUTIONAL CHANGE

The concept of structure assumes different meanings within the context of our work. We discuss two of these meanings here:

- the role of the organizational structure of the Center in encouraging reform, and

- the evolution of new structures for leadership and interaction within the Center and its professional development schools.

■　■　■　■　■　■

WALKING THE TIGHTROPE: AN ORGANIZATIONAL STRUCTURE THAT WORKS

Several years ago, following a presentation about the Center at a conference of representatives of a network of midwest research universities, Henrietta Barnes of Michigan State University commented that at UWM we were "walking a tightrope" in attempting to create reform from within a structure that had neither departmental authority, nor discipline-driven membership. The tightrope is an apt metaphor for the Center and one used frequently since that time. Despite some falls and near misses, there has also developed increasing skill at negotiating the tightrope between the Center and the School of Education departments and other university units, and between the Center and the public schools and community. Indeed, when given the opportunity to recommend to the faculty continuation or revision of the structure of the Center this past spring, the decision was made to maintain the present structure because it serves our programs well.

It is not the case that, on the basis of our experience, we recommend that other institutions reorganize or elect to organize teacher education reform by creating a new interdisciplinary unit. Rather, we extract here some principles that address what we have come to see as significant aspects of organizational structure that can facilitate or impede progress in reform. In our case, the structure may deny us the benefits of an established unit with budgetary and governance rights, but it keeps us collegial and interactive.

STRUCTURAL CONSTRAINTS OR OPPORTUNITIES?

When asked to describe the organizational structure of the Center, we frequently begin with a description of what it is in terms of what it is not. For instance, it is typical to hear the Center described as a unit that is not a department and not a research center, although it does much of the work of each, including scheduling and teaching of classes and encouraging and disseminating the results of research, often collaborative, of its members. The structure is new to our institution and still, after nearly four years, new to us. A view of the organizational structure of the Center for Teacher Education is provided in Figure 1. It is perhaps noteworthy to mention that this figure changes constantly as we continue to debate our vision of the Center and how it fits within existing institutional arrangements.

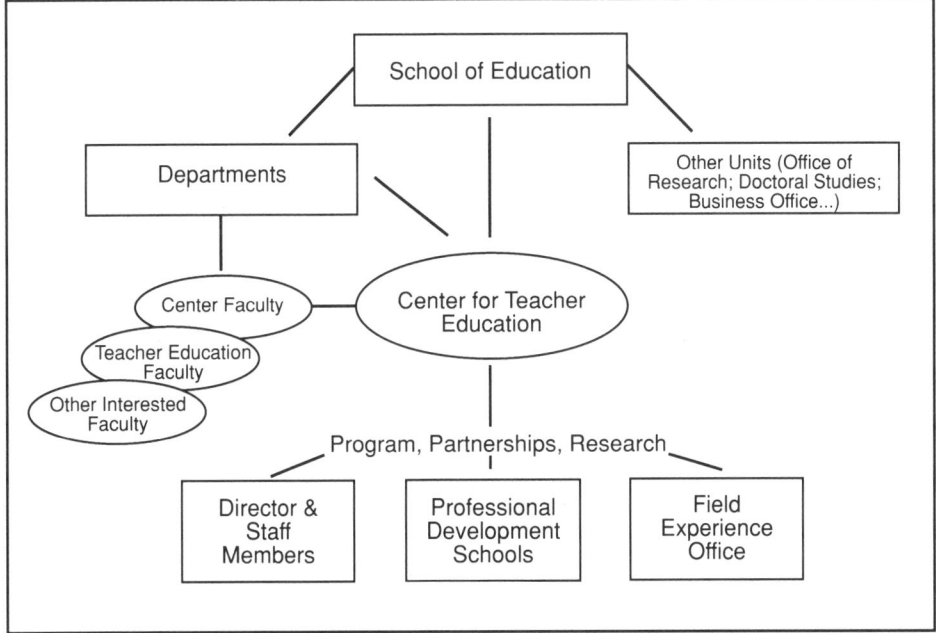

Figure 1. Organizational Structure of the Center for Teacher Education at the University of Wisconsin-Milwaukee.

Briefly, the Center for Teacher Education does not hold governance authority as it is defined in the policies and procedures of the University of Wisconsin-Milwaukee. We do not hire faculty, nor do we grant tenure; all members hold positions in one of five School of Education departments. Curricular authority derives from the School of Education faculty vote to give oversight of teacher education to the Center, but courses exist within departments, and changes in content and structure always require collaborative action between the Center and departmental faculty. Our budget derives from an initial allocation from the Dean and a sharing of resources from the departments. Although we now have a modest instructional budget of our own and supplement our income with grant funds, we do not control faculty salary levels. Instead, the accomplishments of Center members are recognized by recommending to the departments that a portion of the merit money that resides there be allocated to the Center; that determination is made by the departments on an annual basis.

Center faculty, in short, cannot make anybody do anything. We have none of the time-honored means of influencing and shaping university policy. All authority comes from persuasion and creating and sustaining a sense of shared purpose. We depend wholly on the goodwill of our colleagues. As difficult as that can be at times, that is how we have come to believe it ought to be. Institutionalizing change cannot come from fiat, nor from a top-down management style. It must be built through consensus and shared vision and, if it is to last, change must be welcomed, or at least accepted by those who are most directly affected by it.

How Structure Influences Curricular Change
Through Faculty Involvement

To effect curricular change, the Center director and faculty must work with faculty within disciplines and departments. Frequently, an idea will be conceptualized within the Center and then developed in interaction with others; equally as often, the idea may evolve elsewhere and be brought to the Center for its consideration. Indeed this reciprocal interaction is the mode we have adopted to institute most of our changes. It exemplifies the notion that the distinction between "The Center" and "The Departments" is a false one or, as we put it, "We are us." It was not always that way. We share here an incident from our curricular reform efforts that demonstrates how the Center structure has taught us that repeated interaction, feedback, patience, and collaboration are the most effective and appropriate ways to effect change in how teacher educators do business.

From the time of the formation of the original task force, the faculty knew that a major programmatic change that had to take place was reconceptualizing content-specific methods courses. Coursework was delivered in individual units, unconnected to each other, largely unconnected to practice—except as individuals chose to arrange an accompanying clinical placement—and unconnected to other aspects of the program. Faculty teaching the courses were the first to recognize and point this out, and among the first to support the idea of an interdisciplinary Center that would permit change to take place systematically and collaboratively. Yet, at the same time, there was reluctance on the part of many of these faculty to consider new possibilities. Some of this was due to pressure exerted earlier, and not subtly, regarding the "authority" of the Center vis-a-vis program changes, some to the tensions between academic freedom and programmatic integrity, and some to the common concern regarding ownership of "my course."

When the time came to work on this aspect of the program, a group of Center faculty volunteered to prepare a first draft. They worked to design a reasonable proposal to bring to the larger departmental group. They worked with those directly involved in teaching the courses. They asked for input and took back ideas. They talked. And talked. When they were finished, the proposal was brought to the Center faculty where it was worked on some more. Finally, it was distributed to the faculty who needed to act on it. They balked. And balked. The newly appointed permanent director spent an uncomfortable hour at a department meeting hearing about issues that seemed tangential, such as "What about the credits?" "What about teaching load?" and that, fundamentally, reflected distrust and fear. Was the Center taking over faculty or departmental prerogatives? Was the Center going to force a change on faculty?

Although the faculty were assured that this was a working paper, that it was designed to get things going, that what the Center really wanted was faculty involvement and, ultimately, the adoption of what the faculty wanted to do, many did not believe it. The following week, when the meeting began again, the same process was repeated. Finally, the director stood up and ignoring the arguing, lifted up the carefully written, neatly printed document and tore it up. The group began to really consider the issue. A group from within the department was formed and went to work. Later, that group reached out and included practitioners and reworked what they had done. A new approach to integrating subject matter methods was ultimately developed.

In many ways, this was a turning point in the Center's functioning, because it communicated the notion that despite curricular authority being "given" to the Center, its mode of operation was going to be collegial and consensual. Since it is not a department, the organizational structure of the Center mandates adoption of new ideas and approaches by obtaining the approval of others. Instead of viewing this structure as an impediment, we have tried to view it as an opportunity to invite participation in an ongoing and progressively inclusive manner.

How Structure Facilitates the Identification of Common Goals: The Case of Special Education

A continuing challenge in reforming teacher education is how best to integrate the concerns of those faculty who have traditionally been aligned with special education with those in other programs. As a structure for interdisciplinary collaboration, the Center struggled with this concern as a central part of its reform strategy. Some of the very earliest conflicts within the Center focused on the expressed belief that special education was not enough of a focal point in early deliberations, despite its representation on the Center faculty. Alternatively, what also became clear was that at least some faculty in special education believed that it was teacher education programs within curriculum and instruction that needed "fixing," and not programs within their department.

Prior to the Center's establishment, the relationship between special education and other departments was similar to the situation at most institutions of higher education. It was characterized primarily by separate programs and a sense of isolation on the part of the special education faculty. Early on, discussions about special education primarily addressed concerns about the effects of a possible five-year program on special education, about whether this was feasible, and about whether the Center would "force" a decision in other programs that would have dire implications for special education. As program development and reform progressed, however, what began to occur was a serious consideration of how changes in the elementary program, if achieved, would strengthen the core programs in special education by the identification of common goals related to the content of teacher education. No professional core course was developed without the involvement of special education faculty, and these faculty played a major role (through their work in the Center) in working groups that conceptualized the content and process of these courses. When this began to happen, tension subsided, and a sense of shared commitment began to be expressed. These efforts laid the groundwork for all the subsequent interaction, interaction that is today founded on the central belief that our desire for the preparation of good teachers in all aspects of the educational enterprise binds, rather than divides, us.

Further, because there was so much work to do and a limited number of faculty to do it, the Center was interested in identifying those who wanted to get involved and had the skills and desire to do so. Therefore, when it became apparent that the basic course in instruction for the elementary program would be best piloted—and subsequently taught—by a member of the special education faculty, another barrier to recognizing common goals was overcome, and the whole concept of instructional ownership by department began to be replaced with a concern for the teacher education program as a schoolwide phenomenon. Some faculty in special education began to supervise student teachers in the elementary program; a special education faculty member serves as professional development school liaison at one elementary school. This work spans education and is no longer artificially limited only to the isolated preparation of special education teachers. As a result, the contributions of special educators to reform efforts in teacher education have become central to the Center's success.

Once program development was well along within the elementary program, a working group was appointed specifically to reconceptualize special education programs in light of shared goals. Conceptually, the work of this group, which includes members from special education and curriculum and instruction, is to define what is common to and what differentiates the preparation of special education teachers from their counterparts in teacher education as a whole. Working from the professional core developed for elementary education and the conceptual framework for all teacher education programs in the Center, the working group is struggling with the issue of how the roles of special education teachers will be redefined, and how best to prepare special education teachers for those newly defined roles.

To be sure, there was a propensity on the part of some faculty to be accepting of one another across special education and curriculum and instruction. However, the Center provided the catalyst and the reason to come together on a regular basis, to engage in the discussions we wanted but never seemed to find the time to have.

One overt sign of the effect of this collaborative work on the integration of special education into reform efforts involves hiring decisions in the past year. Special education faculty designated one faculty line in the area of mild handicaps, but conceptualized the role of this faculty member as someone who would work cooperatively between special education and the Center for Teacher Education. Thus, an *a priori* commitment was made to conceptualize special education broadly and to identify talented special education faculty who wanted to make a contribution to education as a whole; the position was then advertised in this way. The value of collaboration across disciplines through work with the Center was not limited to this successful search, however. New faculty members in hearing impairment and in severe handicapping conditions also have a broad interest in the quality of teacher preparation and are participating, in various degrees of involvement, in the Center's function and process as a focal point for common concerns regarding how teachers are best prepared.

The result of this once-forced interaction is that it is likely that we will continue to hold the common goal of preparation of good teachers as we work to redefine how special education and classroom teaching are related in the schools. The most important barrier to reaching such a redefinition in terms of teacher preparation has been breached. The dialogue is ongoing, without rancor, and with much goodwill in working toward a common goal. We all find ourselves facing the same problems, whether we prepare special education teachers or elementary and secondary teachers: What constitutes a defensible set of clinical experiences? How do we develop a linked set of instructional experiences? How do we prepare teachers to make independent, sound professional judgments? By dealing with these issues in a collaborative manner, we renew our commitment to the task and gain energy from our joint work toward reform.

CULTURE BUILDING: DEVELOPING NEW PATTERNS OF INTERACTION

The examples above point out how the structure, created to encourage the program and partnership efforts of the Center, was a catalyst for programmatic change. The examples also demonstrate that none of the changes is more important than changes in the working relationships we have developed within the Center, and between the Center and other units, as a part of building a new culture to encourage reform.

Early on, in organizing as the Center for Teacher Education, we adopted familiar academic patterns. We organized into committees and subcommittees; we scheduled all meetings at regular times; we distinguished Center faculty members who were assigned to the Center by their departments from Center affiliates who were faculty with involvement in teacher education who did not hold formal membership on the Center; and we established written procedures to guide our work. However, almost immediately, it became apparent that these patterns did not fit the task of reform, nor did the new structure we had created help facilitate change.

Establishing Group Cohesiveness

What became painfully clear very early on is that we had tasks to do that had no immediate relationship to program and curriculum but had everything to do with the eventual success and implementation of our work. The unspoken question was whether we could actually develop into a cohesive group of faculty members capable of refocusing our lenses, bringing programmatic commit-

ments to teacher education into the foreground, and placing departmental allegiances in the background. More to the point, could we really create a community
that transcended departmental politics, without at the same time slipping into the
defensive posture of a department ourselves? And could we convince our colleagues who were not Center members but who, without question, were central to
the delivery of a consistent teacher education program, to do the same?

Given the tentative nature of our mandate and the three-
year time period we had been allotted, it seemed certain that this was our real work,
and what followed can perhaps best be characterized as a series of tests to see how
common our goal was in reality. Of the many problems we encountered in this regard, three stand out:

- how to tolerate each other as we developed a sense of interpersonal
  honesty, and how to expand our tolerance for each other;

- how to limit our tendencies to complain to our friends and departmental colleagues regarding Center dynamics; and

- how to be patient as the Center dealt with issues that might not appear
  to affect all departments involved in teacher education equally in the
  short run.

These were the battles of trust we naively embarked on
in the early days of the Center's existence and that have formed the basis for our
current functioning.

Lessons from Persistence and Commitment

Some of us had sat for years on other university commit-
tees with Center faculty and others were newcomers; some prejudices had been
formed by experience, others by rumor. We were sitting with public school people
who knew nothing of us. At first we tested each other for style—leadership style,
group interaction style, and the like. Could we learn to tolerate each other's styles,
and would styles change over time? We spent a good deal of time together, biweekly
in full meetings, and most of us also saw each other weekly in subcommittee meetings.
Our physical environment did not promote interdepartmental interaction; separated by floors and with no common meeting areas, we found spending so much
time together with faculty from other departments a new experience.

For the Center to succeed, the group had to be able to
work effectively, and that meant not expending energy complaining about each

other as individuals. From the start, a decision was made to reach consensus rather than to push issues to a vote; in retrospect that was a critical tone-setting decision, although it did not spare us growing pains. It is still the case that votes are taken only on rare occasions when university or state regulations require it. Building consensus on group actions encouraged not only discussion but also collaborative interaction.

Those interactions were intense. Since we sought new ways to interact, we decided that a deliberate and honest airing of worries, problems, and perceptions of the Center was the strategy to adopt. In time, a subtle shift seemed to take place. It may be that we realized that there was a great deal of work to do, or perhaps, that we recognized a real opportunity to create a coherent teacher education program. Center meetings were emotionally exhausting; we never knew who would take the opportunity to lay bare their feelings that week. The analogy to therapy began to be heard, and the analogy hit hardest, perhaps, at our first retreat. Prompted by our dean's concern for quicker progress, we argued about our work, our goals, and our future. As a result, we grew more connected and more interdependent. That early retreat seemed to be a turning point.

At the same time, it became apparent that something different was taking place within the School of Education as a whole. For the first time in anyone's recent memory, more people seemed to know what was going on in all corners of the school than ever before. Both within and outside the Center, people were making connections across departments in ways that had never happened previously. Interaction with departments and departmental concerns was virtually assured since all departments and programs are represented on the Center, and since this coordination was built in by design, it seemed to be starting to work. Things positive and negative were not remaining within departments to be mulled over or complained about. It seemed that nothing went on that was not known by everyone before long and that nothing went on regarding the Center that was not quickly known by one of its members.

One outcome of this new environment was that rumors began to move more swiftly, and came quickly to the Center's attention. The Center faculty dealt with what it was hearing both collectively and individually. Everything was fair game; topics ranged from departments that were rumored to be exasperated with the Center to correcting misrepresentations of the Center's position on various issues in other parts of the School. Rumor control was hard work. Working in a more communicative, open environment was exciting and a goal worth working toward. And this sense of communication extended beyond the School itself, manifesting itself in the processes used to identify professional development schools and to redesign our relationships with all our clinical sites through our newly organized Office of Field Experiences.

The open style of communication and new socialization patterns occurring within the Center were not easily transferred, however. It took time to learn how best to include colleagues who were not formally members in an active way. Our early work was done largely in isolation; we seemed to need to build our own group style first. During the second year of operation, however, we began to look outward. At first we opened our subcommittees to encourage Center affiliates to participate on projects. We assiduously interviewed our colleagues regarding the development of new methods courses; our second retreat was designed for members and affiliates alike. People began to speak of coordination of program sequence, of writing curriculum across programs for general courses to provide multiple exemplars, of pulling together. We have used this strategy of building trust and moving outward in establishing our relationships with our colleagues in the professional development schools as well.

Our meetings are still intense, but we are aware that something new is taking place, something serious, relating to how we work together. While attributions about our progress to date are difficult to make, we do think at the least that it has to do with persistence and openness, and with taking the time to grow. At best, it has to do with the realization that it may be possible to share a common goal after all.

EVOLVING PATTERNS

When the Center for Teacher Education was created it was viewed as an interdepartmental faculty unit, charged with looking after the welfare of the teacher education program. Today, the Center's shape and makeup have changed. In the beginning it was yet another unit with membership rules for exclusion and inclusion, regular meeting times, and a structure that consisted of committees and subcommittees. We now view the Center as not only an experiment in teacher education reform, but also as an experiment in organizational structure and leadership. There are no longer permanent subcommittees; rather, there are working groups that deal with particular purposes, open to all who wish to participate; these groups are disbanded when the task is complete. Membership, too, is more fluid. There are no longer distinctions between Center faculty members and Center affiliates. While we still have Center faculty, mostly for purposes of ensuring program representation, we have expanded the membership and encouraged the attendance of all. Today, Center meetings are regularly attended by many whose names are not on the official list and, on a sporadic basis, by others interested in the issue to be discussed. Assistant professors, who were "protected" from inclusion in the Center in its early days, are now active participants as Center faculty members and members of working groups. In the beginning, we used our modest budget to

	Pre-Center	1986-1987	1990-1991
Membership	All teacher education activity located in individual departments (e.g.,C & I, Ex. Ed., Ed. Psych.). Approvals for changes made through hierarchical structures.	As specified in enabling legislation; representational Center Faculty & Center Affiliates. Expressed concern about Assistant Professor service on Center.	Fluid membership; open attendance. Additional at-large members; administrative expertise added. Many Assistant Professors.
Procedure	Decisions by vote.	Consensus. ━━━━	
Structure	No interdisciplinary structure outside existing schoolwide committees.	Center committees and subcommittees. Connections to Schoolwide Committees.	Working Groups with Open Membership and Timeline Defined by Task.
Tasks	Any changes to be made determined within individual units. No schoolwide focus on reform.	Create Office of Field Experience. Establish PDS. Work on Program. ━ Model of Change ━	New Program(s). Cohorts and Themes. Academic, Clinical syntheses. Monitoring Progress. Ongoing Reform.
Relationships with Others	Formal relationships through governance structures.	Center Faculty. Center Affiliates. Formal Structures.	Reciprocal interaction between Center and Departments. Permeable boundaries for ideas, members.

Key:
C & I	Curriculum and Instruction
Ex. Ed.	Exceptional Education
Ed. Psych.	Educational Psychology
PDS	Professional Development School

Figure 2. Evolving Patterns of Interaction and Leadership in the Center for Teacher Education.

■   ■   ■   ■   ■   ■

release only Center faculty members from a course to permit them to work with the Center. Today, releases are tied to specific tasks, and many of them are given to faculty who are involved in the work of the Center but who are not officially designated as Center faculty. Trends characterizing the movement toward greater democratization of participation and decision making are illustrated in Figure 2.

Walking the tightrope is often a painstaking and frustrating process. From the beginning we grappled with problems of how to negotiate the delicate balance between the Center and the departments. That this is an ongoing consideration was recently made clear to us again when the School of Education held a retreat to discuss its mission and future initiatives. Despite the many positive changes that have occurred in how the Center is viewed in the School, faculty still voiced concerns about the Center's future development, about its role in relation to the departments and their authority, and about its share of resources. The conversation affirmed that the Center represents a new mode of interaction, and one that is still uncomfortable for some and of concern to other faculty members. We must continue to listen, to examine our structure, and to recommend changes that will keep us flexible, alert, and able to address the ongoing tasks.

■

COLLABORATION AS REFORM STRATEGY

Innovation of the sort created through the Center for Teacher Education calls for a supportive environment, one in which both new ideas and persistent hard work can flourish. From its inception, the Center worked to build that supportive environment through its reliance on collaboration as a reform strategy. Many aspects of the above discussion on how structure has influenced our development and actions point out the simple and enormously important notion that our structure mandated that we work together across disciplines within the Center; across departments within the School; across units of the university; and between the university and the public schools. While we are convinced that the positive outcomes in program reform and professional development school implementation that we have brought about thus far are directly due to that collaboration and, in particular, to our collaborative structural model, we cannot claim that this mode of interaction has been without its frustrations or easy to achieve. Indeed, as the word "collaboration" invades all aspects of the reform literature, it becomes more and more clear that those who are involved in these efforts need to articulate what is meant by this concept and then specify how it is developed. That is the intent of the next section of this chapter. Since we have already described the process we engaged in over time to build our working relationships, we emphasize here the opportunities our way of working offers us and provide some suggestions that we have developed based on our collective experience about how to nurture and maintain collaboration.

INTERDISCIPLINARY INTERACTION AND
DECISION MAKING

One of the most exciting aspects of working across departments within the Center is that fresh perspectives are brought to a similar agenda. In part, at least, those perspectives emerge from our disciplines and their methodologies, as well as from our personal characteristics and philosophies. We have been forced to develop a tolerance that faculty groups often fail to develop, and our discussions are flavored by the language and thought processes of philosophy, psychology, and curriculum theory. In developing a community, we also try to keep in mind our affiliation to our departments. Long after we developed a sense of group as a Center, we continue to wonder how a new idea will be received on our departmental home turf. In other words, we bring different ideas to the Center, develop a consensual approach, and then examine our own perceptions and approaches in light of the expectations and concerns of our departmental colleagues. That has been a useful tension. By design, the Center builds those tensions to enable it to serve as a stimulus for ongoing change.

We have also benefitted from another advantage of working across disciplines and departments. Within any Department of Educational Psychology or Department of Curriculum and Instruction, for example, there are vast differences in approach and perspective, as well as numerous similarities that emerge from training and content. Thus, within a departmental context, though one is among colleagues, one is not always among peers. Within the Center structure, faculty have been able to develop a sense of loyalty to a different peer group, one that emerges from a commitment to common goals. While teacher education is broadly the context for that affiliation, it is more the identification of a peer group based on our consensus building that has provided many with the sense of belonging that encourages not only collective accomplishments but individual growth, growth that we take into independent projects, as well as bring to our collaborative writing and programmatic work. We have come to support each other in ways that go far beyond our reform work.

BUILDING A COLLABORATIVE SPIRIT INSIDE AND OUTSIDE THE UNIVERSITY

The creation of the Center was a turning point since it provided a forum in which collaborative efforts not only could, but had to, take place for our mission to be addressed. But, at the beginning, it was only a facilitative shell, and there were those who believed that if we were to educate future teachers to be collegial, interactive, and cooperative, we, too, had to learn how to do that so that we might model those practices for our students.

Our collaborative efforts in the Center for Teacher Education have taken place in two settings, one internal to the university and the other reaching out from it. In the first, we have collaborated with our faculty colleagues within the School of Education and across the campus in designing and teaching new approaches to educating future teachers, in facilitating the adoption of the new approach, and in producing scholarly work. In the second, we have extended our effort to identifying and interacting with new colleagues in the public schools and in the community at large. In both settings, our interactions and efforts are public.

Collaboratively, we have chosen the direction of preparing prospective teachers to work in the urban schools and to look at the teaching career from a holistic perspective that begins when one says, "Maybe I'd like to be a teacher," and ends when one retires. That holistic viewpoint means we must address both preservice education and staff development simultaneously. And because of our urban commitment, most of the clinical settings for our work, including our professional development schools, are located in a large, urban, bureaucratic school district that is itself undergoing reform. All this work—creating new programs, helping develop partnership strategies, and managing connections between the university and the schools—is being conducted in collaboration with others.

Although collaboration was the obvious strategy for our task, we have come to employ it—real collaboration—as slowly as any group of academics who work in a research university that rewards individual accomplishment. And while teacher education has always been described as a collaborative endeavor, it has not always been conducted that way. We had to develop our collaborative strategy and persist even when it seemed as if the group process was too slow, too painful, and too hard.

ACKNOWLEDGING THE NEED FOR SUPPORT

The frustrations of collaborative work are often great—it is often easier to forge ahead or to take falls on one's own. When one acts independently, there is no one else to wait for, no one else to pull you in new directions that you had not anticipated, no one else to explain your ideas to, no one else with whom to work. And yet, that, of course, is it. There is no one else to wait for, no one else with whom to work. The joys outweigh the frustrations, but we have had to learn to recognize and to share both sets of feelings.

As academics, most of us thrive on the stimulation inherent in discussing, debating, and exploring with others an issue of mutual concern—worrying about it, taking it apart, adding the new twists that come only from another mind—and finding both confirmation and expansion in the results. As people who care about seeing ideas come alive, we continue to appreciate a process that permits us to feel we can make a difference if we work together to effect change. As individuals, we feel the satisfaction of completing a task and of sharing a sense of completion with our peers.

GIVING THE PROCESS TIME

Collaboration, however, takes more time than many seem to want to give it. Consensus building and partnership are processes that take energy and time "up front," and many of us are not used to operating that way. Our usual approach says: "Just get it done." "Just do it because I said so." The fact that this approach only seems to work for a short while seems to be ignored—in childrearing, in teaching, in preparing teachers, and in managing schools. Change, too, is often threatening, and when people are either pulled into it screaming or run into it without looking, it fails to work. We must continually remind ourselves and each other that what we are doing is worth the effort. We have recently learned to build support sessions directly into our efforts.

Over the past years we have become convinced that to reach our goals we must be invested in listening to people's concerns, addressing them if possible, staying flexible, and, above all, building a working consensus. Because people do what they want to do, unless consensus is reached change does not take place. What our work seems to be saying is that collaboration is the appropriate, the logical, the sensible strategy for making change work. It is not just pragmatic. It is also intellectually defensible. It feels right. But collaboration must be nurtured in a deliberate way.

SOME FINAL OBSERVATIONS

Where does the UWM Center for Teacher Education go from here? Change is a messy business and, so, we will probably continue to go in several directions at once as we have been doing. The current agenda includes specifying the details of how the needs of particular programs will be addressed within the context of our programmatic reform model. We must also determine how to implement the concept of cohort groups in an urban, commuter campus with many transfer students, postbaccalaureate students, and working students. We have nearly completed changes in methods courses and have already begun addressing changes in how clinical experiences are conceptualized. This means more work with academic departments and schools, smoothing the way, creating consensus, addressing concerns, and balancing the values of academic freedom and program integrity.

Continuing to develop coherent models of working with urban professional development schools, and exploring new ways of actualizing the commitment to partnership, are other priorities. A number of challenges to our efforts are already apparent. Can we make our desire to have a clinical laboratory for the issues of preparation of preservice teachers compatible with the need in the buildings for developing staff and restructuring professional roles? Theoretically, these needs are interdependent; we must address issues of practice concurrently with preparation if schools are to become better places to work and places that work better. We continue to struggle with the challenges of preparing teacher education students for complex urban schools.

Perhaps one of the greatest challenges, following the initial years of work and the experiencing of some success, is how to maintain our enthusiasm, productivity, and spirit of inquiry. By way of conclusion, we will share a few insights about institutionalizing change through a collaborative structure that may have some generalizability from our experience to those of others.

BUILD A STRUCTURE TO SUPPORT CHANGE

We have proceeded structurally because our intent is to reform programs meaningfully and in ways that outlast those of us who are putting our energies into this end of the task. When the latest reform wave passes over, we still want to be in the business of creating prospective teachers who will enter the profession prepared to begin their work and able to grow professionally over a period of many years. Structural change does not mean adopting the specific organizational structure the Center represents. It means moving more slowly than some would like toward a goal and taking time to stop along the way and invite others to accompany us. We believe that collaboration will benefit our programs, our students, and, ultimately, the children our teachers will teach.

IMPLEMENT AND NURTURE THE COLLABORATIVE PROCESS

One of the lessons of our experience to date is that we need to use modeling as a strategy for ourselves, as well as for our students. Part of what we are learning to do as we institute change through the Center is to model, for our colleagues, collaborative problem solving. Convincing through persuasion rather than imposition can be difficult, but we are often surprised at its results. Being open to others' suggestions, rather than moving doggedly ahead on our own road with blinders on, has benefitted us in some concrete ways, as we discovered with the redesign of our methods courses. We are not concerned with "bringing along" recalcitrant faculty; we are very concerned with learning more about the process of "including in" our colleagues.

Another implication of using collaborative process as the mode of work is that it requires a different kind of leadership, as well as different patterns of work. Leaders need to find ways to support reform efforts, both fiscally, emotionally, and through the application of administrative patterns that rely more on sharing of information and roles and less on control and a hierarchical organization. In the Center, we are still involved in the evolution of these new strategies. We have learned, however, that empowering ourselves to make meaningful change requires leaders who are comfortable in facilitating the work of others and in sharing authority and decision making with others while still providing vision.

An additional outcome of our experimentation in collaborative interaction has been the positive effect it has had on our relationship with the professional development school staffs. We have gained credibility by being able to indicate that we, too, are attempting to redefine roles and to develop different patterns of work.

Finally, and most importantly, we are enjoying our work. The positive feelings that come from collaborative interaction and productivity are an important part of changing teacher education and the teaching profession in ways that will be meaningful and lasting. Facing challenges together and exploring how to address them is a new model for faculty in schools of education, and it is that model we believe will ultimately make the real difference in the teachers we produce and the type of profession we become.

■

REFERENCES

The Holmes Group. (1990). *Tomorrow's schools: Principles for the design of professional development schools.* East Lansing, MI: Author.

Pasch, S. H., & Pugach, M. C. (1990). Collaborative planning in urban professional development schools. *Contempory Education, 61,* 135-143.

Schug, M., Pugach, M., & Pasch, S. (1988, February). *Programmatic coherence through interdisciplinary responsibility: The UWM Center for Teacher Education,* American Association of Colleges for Teacher Education Annual Meeting, New Orleans.

Writing Committee of the Task Force on Teacher Education. (1986). *A proposal for a Center for Teacher Education.* Milwaukee, WI: University of Wisconsin-Milwaukee School of Education.

■ ■ ■ ■ ■ ■

CASE TWO: THE ROLE OF AN EXTERNAL CONSULTANT IN FOSTERING FACULTY DEVELOPMENT

7

JOYCE PUTNAM

Overview. One of the most critical aspects of teacher education reform is the faculty's capacity to understand both the dynamics of change and their own roles within an evolutionary process. Redesigning the teacher education curriculum requires that new visions and possibilities be constructed by the faculty who will create and sustain the innovations that result. Such redesign efforts, therefore, depend on faculty who have ownership of the new curriculum. Developing new visions is critical to the change process and may require exposure to different approaches to educating teachers. But faculty development must go beyond conceptualizing the curriculum. Faculty often need support in recognizing institutional barriers that may prevent innovative programs from being adopted. The case description that follows discusses the role of an external consultant in addressing conceptual, institutional, and political issues involved in reforming teacher education. ■

■ ■ ■ ■ ■ ■ ■

As teacher educators attempt to change their programs to respond to society's needs for teachers in an information era, they are realizing the difficulty and complexity of the job. Because the task is complicated, several factors must be addressed including both what needs to be done and the process used to accomplish these ends. This process needs to support change that will be both in-depth and long term. As can be seen from the chapter titles in this monograph, a number of foci direct the process used for bringing about successful change in teacher education programs (e.g., change through staff development, change through restructuring the governance of program). This chapter describes a case of change in teacher education programs in which an external consultant helped stimulate faculty to develop new concepts of teacher education and facilitated change in institutional structures to support these new visions.

The chapter is organized into two sections: the first section describes the role of the external consultant in the change process; and the second discusses themes and principles that undergird the building of relationships to support the change effort. The conclusion includes the consultant's insights about key factors for change.

The change described in this chapter took place at a conventional mid-sized state college. Education programs at the college are housed in the School of Education and Related Professional Studies (SERPS), which is composed of eight departments, has about 90 full-time faculty equivalents, and admits about 1,000 students per year. The Departments of Health and Physical Education; Technology; Home Economics; Curriculum and Instruction: Elementary/Early Childhood Education; Secondary Education Foundations; and Special Educational Services/Instruction each offer several alternative undergraduate certification programs. The Departments of Reading/Speech Correction and Educational Administration offer graduate degrees. The SERPS is headed by a dean who works directly with the chairs of the eight departments.

At the time the program redesign was initiated, the school was headed by an interim dean who had a long history as a faculty leader. Prior to her role as interim dean she had served as chair of the Curriculum and Instruction: Elementary/Early Childhood Education Department. After the initiation of this change project, when the new dean was hired, the interim dean once again became a member of the faculty and took on the responsibility of directing the redesign component of the grant.

To bring about program change, the interim dean developed a long-range plan. Her long-range planning culminated in:

- the hiring of four new faculty,

- the generation of grant funds for faculty and staff development,

- the creation of a link with the American Association of Colleges for Teacher Education,

- the successful search for a new dean, and

- the hiring of an external consultant.

All of these outcomes were important to the successful initiation of the redesign effort. For example, two of the new faculty took active leadership roles in the redesign effort. The grant funds provided resources for support of necessary redesign functions including: faculty study time, travel to national conferences, and travel to observe the operation of nontraditional teacher educational programs. Only minimal support for these activities was present before the grant. The interim dean saw a need for relationships to be created with professionals at other colleges and universities as a means for the professional development of the faculty. She decided that AACTE could provide the best connections to the multiple resources needed. She also believed that by working through AACTE, the college could avoid political problems related to forming a partnership with any single nearby university. She saw AACTE as a resource for facilitating change.

A representative from the national AACTE organization worked with the interim dean to set up a framework for three faculty retreats. The representative suggested that *Knowledge Base for the Beginning Teacher* (KBBT) would provide a foundation for beginning the staff development deliberations. The representative also identified KBBT authors to act as speakers at the retreats. Finally, the AACTE representative identified a person who would act as the external consultant for program redesign. The external consultant was initially hired to provide: (1) activities for three days of deliberations among faculty, which occurred after two days of KBBT authors/speakers; (2) assistance in planning the second and third retreats; and (3) leadership for the faculty and administrators in the planning of the second and third retreats. After agreeing to work on the retreats the external consultant was asked to consider a longer-term relationship, one that would involve the external consultant in several trips to the college over a year's time for the purpose of leading the faculty in their redesign effort. However, no agreement was reached because: (1) the interim dean needed more information about the consultant's ability to work with the faculty, (2) a new dean was to be hired within a couple of months, and (3) the consultant wanted more information about the capacity of the faculty and administration and the nature of the redesign expectations.

The new dean was hired and began work during the second summer retreat. His participation in the second retreat provided the initial support for the redesign effort. Faculty questions about what the new dean would and would not support were quickly answered. At the end of the second summer retreat the interim dean and new dean together recruited the external consultant to work with the SERPS for at least one year.

The external consultant actually worked for two years (1988-90) at the SERPS. The first year involved the three originally scheduled week-long retreats and frequent on-site work by the consultant. In September 1989, the external consultant began to visit the campus from three to five days every three weeks. The consultant worked 10- to 14-hour days with a wide variety of faculty and administrators. (See Figure 1.) She also spent several days, between each visit to the campus, preparing materials and reviewing work done by the faculty.

In general, six months were spent exploring and getting ready to design structures for the new teacher education programs. About nine months were spent on writing programs, and another nine months were spent on the piloting process and making the revisions that were needed for full implementation of the program courses. At the beginning of the third year the new programs were implemented in three departments. They were approved through the formal governance system. (See Figure 2.)

The external consultant's role was to provide leadership for faculty development and program redesign. She saw herself as a facilitator for change. Over the two years she worked to: (1) create readiness for change (Figure 2, Points 1-5); (2) organize faculty to complete conceptual program redesign work (Figure 2, Points 6-8); (3) facilitate the faculty's interest and ability to study the impact of piloted courses (Figure 2, Point 9); and (4) facilitate faculty revisions of courses and field experiences. Following is a description of how the external consultant was involved in the change process.

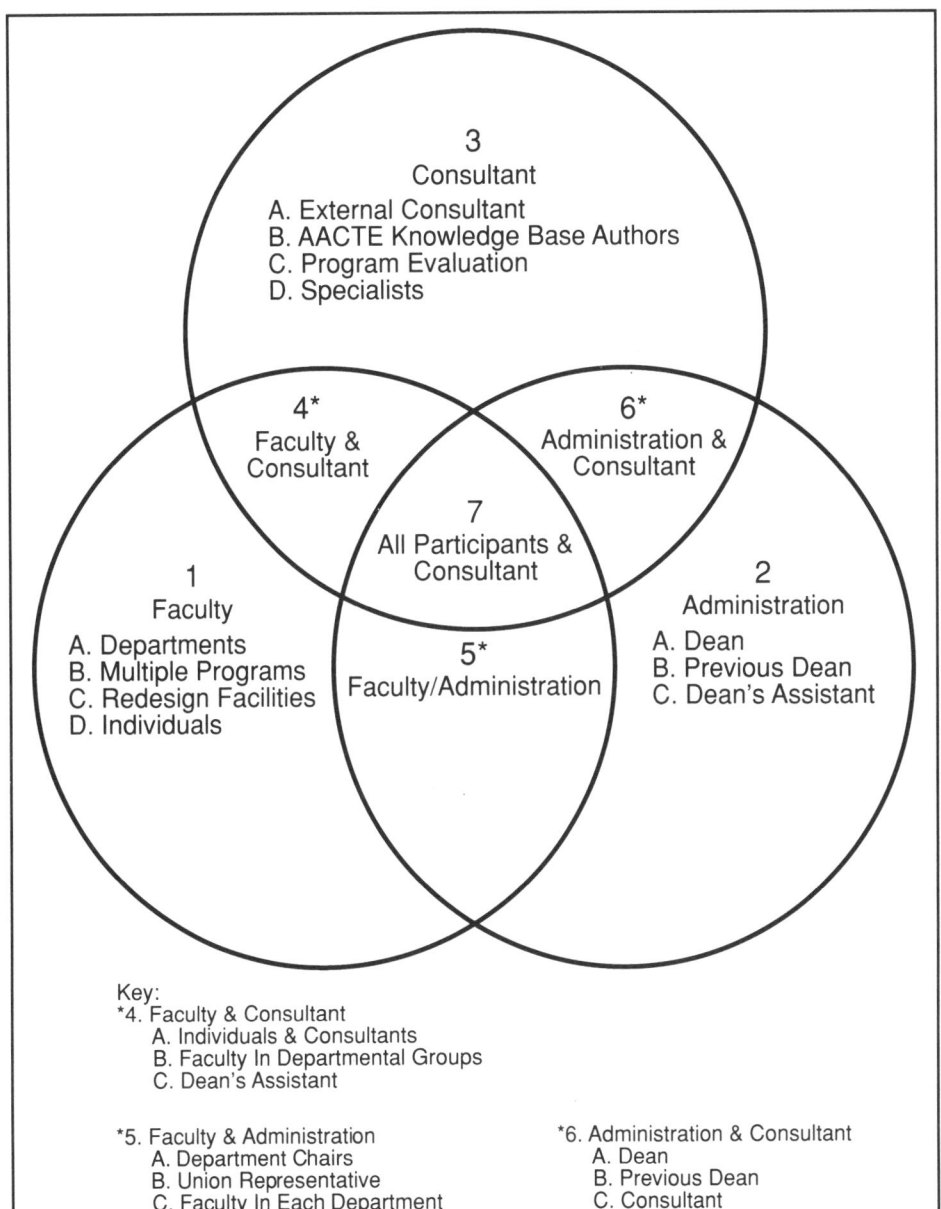

Figure 1. Groups Involved in Redesign Efforts

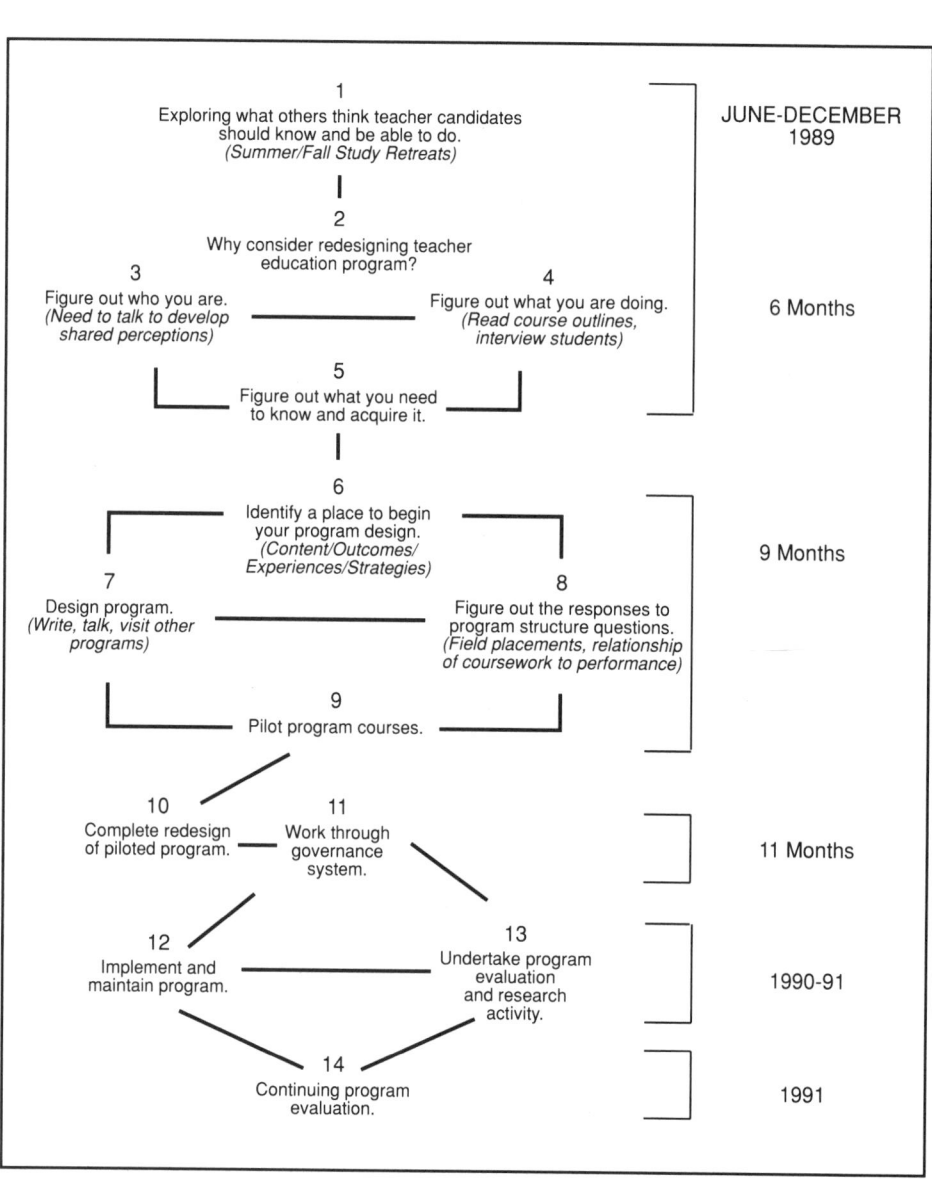

Figure 2. Program Redesign

■

THE PROCESS OF CHANGE

The external consultant perceived her role over the two-year period of time as one of fostering group movement through three change phases: data gathering, moving the redesign process along, and piloting and implementing redesigned programs. Barnes (1989) hypothesized that change in teacher education could be examined from the perspective of 12 factors that interact in a given teacher education site. In this description, these influences have been organized to help explain the three phases of change that occurred.

The influences included in the explanation of the first phase of change, *Data Gathering*, are: expectations and first impressions; history and norms; administrative and faculty leadership; assessing faculty capacity, efficacy, and perspectives; faculty assessment of current programs; and conditions and capacity for change. In the second phase, *Moving the Redesign Process Along*, influences include: program definition, initiating capacity building, academic organizational change, and strategies. The influences included in the third phase, *Piloting and Implementing Redesigned Programs*, are: developing capacity, creating conditions, and completing trials connected with studies of practice. Descriptions of these three phases of change and the external consultant's role follow.

CHANGE PHASE I: DATA GATHERING

The first phase of the change process, Data Gathering, was initiated by the external consultant for two purposes. First, the consultant needed to develop her own understanding of the institution's context and goals and her role. Second, the local faculty and administrators, along with the consultant, needed to create shared understandings about the nature of their current programs and the need for redesign. Data gathering and analysis would contribute to these goals.

The external consultant's goal was to construct an understanding of the context, as interpreted from her perspective, as well as an understanding of the faculty and administration's perspectives of that same context. That

■ ■ ■ ■ ■ ■ ■

is, she needed to construct both an outsider's understanding and an understanding of the insider's perspective. Thus, she set about to identify:

- the key personnel (or stakeholders) in the effort,

- the nature of the role AACTE's national representative and the interim dean had in mind for her,

- the contribution of her role to the overall reform plan,

- the interim dean's expectations for long range outcomes,

- the interim dean's perspective about the faculty and context, and

- the specifics of the plans that had been made for the three retreats and the amount of room there was for change within the established plans.

Data collection processes included participant observation methods and surveys as a means of looking systematically at the faculty's perspectives. Two questionnaires were used: the Exxon Survey created by Barnes (1989) on faculty perceptions of change factors and a questionnaire created by the National Center for Research on Teacher Education at Michigan State University that assessed faculty views of teaching and learning. Data from about 30 percent of the total faculty were received. The low rate of return was congruent with group nonparticipation and isolation norms in place at the time the redesign work began. The external consultant also talked extensively with faculty, students, and administrators and read a variety of local documents. The documents included course outlines for all current courses offered in three programs, the student teaching handbook, and program descriptions.

Expectations and First Impressions

Generating first impressions and identifying expectations was the consultant's first task. The external consultant began this by becoming involved in planning for the three staff development retreats with the AACTE representative responsible for working with the SERPS. The initial planning was conducted by phone as the local faculty, interim dean, and AACTE consultants for the retreats were located around the country. The route of conversations led from the representative to workshop speakers, to the interim dean, to a college program evaluator, to a Department of Administration faculty member, to a Department of Special Education faculty member, to a member of the faculty at the external consultant's own university, and around again. Each conversation provided additional clarity about the project. The consultant's questions contributed to others' clarifying their own roles in the endeavor, their expectations, their commitments, and the plans for the retreats.

Based on the initial data collected, the external consultant found that:

- the interim dean was the primary stakeholder in the reform,

- the external consultant was expected to create her own role,

- the interim dean was the primary local leader in the reform effort,

- the interim dean wanted three new teacher education programs created, and

- the faculty were just becoming involved in the idea of a local redesign effort.

Concerning the plans for the retreats, the consultant found that:

- the proposed format for the initial retreat was incongruent with the interim dean's expectations for outcomes,

- conceptual links among the topics for the speakers for the retreats were not apparent,

- local faculty leadership beyond the interim dean was not visible, and

- plans were tentative enough that there was room to make changes.

The understandings developed during the initial series of conversations served as the basis for the interim dean, AACTE representative, and the external consultant to work out a plan for the first retreat that, to some extent, suited everyone's needs. The three also agreed that the SERPS faculty would participate in the planning of the second and third retreats.

A second phase of the data collection began when participants met for the first time at the first retreat. This phase of assessment is characterized by questions about expectations and first impressions from both the consultant and faculty. The consultant asked herself context and organizational questions such as: Who are these people? Who currently provides curriculum, organizational, and programmatic leadership for the college? Who will/can/could provide leadership from within the school/department/group? What do the faculty think about their current program/teaching/teacher candidate outcomes? How do these professors spend their professional time? How are they organized? What is the reputation of this SERPS? Who can provide support in ways that the faculty will feel rewarded? She looked for answers to these questions in conversations with faculty, administrators, students, and local residents.

The faculty had a different set of questions they wanted answered, which included: What are we doing? Who is in the group? How will I be treated? What is expected of me? Who is this consultant? What does she know? What kind of leadership will she provide? What will she think of me/us? What is the worst thing that could happen to me if this "redesign" actually happens? Who are these AACTE authors? Who made them the experts? And, can we trust the consultant? These questions provided a means for all to make sense initially out of the retreat experiences. Continuing conversations and collective reading of common materials led to additional shared understandings.

It should be noted that answers to these questions changed over time. As members of the group got more information about each other and studied and developed shared understandings, their understandings relative to the questions also changed. As the external consultant and faculty progressed through the redesign effort, the questions changed even further. For example, when the curriculum started being written, people no longer asked "Are we going to do this?" but instead began to ask two new questions: "How will I get what I teach into the new curriculum?" and "How will we get some people to change?"

The external consultant's first impression of the faculty was that there was a very diverse range of professional values among the faculty. The faculty's response to the AACTE speakers ranged from "these people don't know anything" to "we are really out of touch with professional education research and theory." Their first responses to the external consultant ranged from hostile and self-protective to friendly and reflective.

History and Norms

As the SERPS members and the external consultant worked together during the first three retreats, more elaborate understandings about the context were developed. Information about the history and norms of the institution provided three types of understandings. First was the understanding about what contributed to the School's current state. Second was an understanding of the images that faculty, students, and local graduates held about the programs.

Third was an understanding of the norms for the way people talked to each other, defined relationships and expectations, and promoted or interfered with change. These understandings helped the consultant to identify the ethos of the faculty group.

Information that helped form the initial understandings about the school's current state focused primarily on the role of state government in teacher education. During the period from 1981 to 1986, state colleges were asked to make yearly changes. Rilling (1990) illustrates the sense of utter frustration these changes created when she says, "With little or no time to consider the wisdom or impact related to the substance of the changes, nor the best strategies for implementation, all moves focused on change in distribution of and credit requirements to meet numerical mandates" (p. 7). Thus, for several years the faculty, without their input, had seen their courses depleted and the remaining credits reorganized to meet state mandates. From the faculty's perspective, all of this change resulted primarily in a reduction of education credits with the remaining credits used to meet state mandates. Within these mandates the faculty worked hard to maintain what they could of their original courses (Rilling, 1990).

On the one hand, the faculty had seen a lot of change in program structure and credits that resulted in the loss of time with teacher candidates. On the other hand, they had worked hard to keep what was originally taught in their education program since they believed that it was good. To the external consultant, as an outsider, at first glance it appeared that the programs were stationary and traditional. A second glance revealed that a lot of change had taken place. The change was mostly in numbers of credits but also included the loss of collegiality, up-to-date course content, and creative course instruction. More importantly, it felt like a lot of change to the faculty.

The norm for faculty interaction was primarily one of isolation. Faculty reported that "once" they had been a group that was concerned about current K-12 teaching methods and learning to teach strategies. They came to understand that they had lost that close-knit collegiality and now interacted with each other only when faculty meetings were called by the department chairs. They reported that they saw the purpose of the department meetings as the time to give out administrative information and, on occasion, to inform faculty about a crisis. In a crisis situation, the faculty responded by doing whatever was asked by the administrator. In other situations, they talked but went off "to do their own thing." One faculty member, reflecting on his experience at the School, described the situation as one where faculty came to campus to read their mail, hold required office hours, and teach their classes. Life at the SERPS was untroubled for the most part and things ran pretty smoothly. The primary decision that needed to be made each semester was who would teach what and when. The system for deciding these questions was well established and followed by department chairs.

The faculty's isolation from each other and other professionals perpetuated the status quo. Few faculty attended conferences, fewer presented papers. Most faculty held secondary jobs or were engaged in education-related consulting. Basic needs for affiliation and achievement were met primarily with contacts outside of the college. The norm for what constituted professional activity was one of full-time teaching and/or supervision of student teachers. The SERPS did not assign time, on a regular basis, for research and service. The institutional structure of the School did not include any committee structure that supported research and renewal or evaluation of programs. For example, the consultant found that while numerous paper changes and course title changes had been sent through the curriculum committee, these changes were not developed by or necessarily supported by faculty but were handled primarily by the administrators. The reason the administrators did not consult faculty was that they wanted to avoid increasing tension within the faculty group. Thus, they perceived their actions as protective and supportive of the faculty. For example, one year the chair of a department had rewritten course outlines to meet state requirements. At the beginning of this current redesign effort, some faculty indicated they had not seen the particular edition of course outlines developed by the department chair.

The external consultant decided to challenge the professional activity norm. She designed a plan to organize a group that would study the change process. The intent was to provide support for scholarship for two of the new faculty (heavily involved in the change process), interim dean, and others; to challenge the norm about faculty load time; and to provide a basis for the School to disseminate its change process to others in the field. Faculty involved in the research project did receive load time for their work once the request was made and the study was started.

Analysis of the Exxon Survey data indicated that faculty thought that the political organization and the historical and current context inhibited and constrained change in the teacher education curriculum (Putnam, 1990). These data helped provide an insider's sense of the overall effect of the state's actions on what appeared to have once been an energetic, creative faculty.

Administrator and Faculty Leadership

At the outset of the project, the leadership for change consisted of the interim dean and two special education faculty. By the end of the first retreat, the consultant identified one first-year faculty member who appeared to have leadership potential. By the end of the second retreat one other person, newly hired, seemed also to have the capacity to provide leadership for change. Immediately on his arrival, he began to support local leadership in the change effort.

At the onset of the redesign effort, the three department chairs were either not involved or overtly worked against the redesign. At the end of the first year of the redesign effort, two new chairs were selected. One of the new chairs had provided the leadership for his department's redesign and continued to do so into the second year of the project. The second chair was involved in the department's redesign efforts initially in a nonsupportive role. As the year progressed, he provided support. As chair, he worked to clarify what people wanted to do and provided the necessary changes in schedules and procedures for implementing the pilots of new courses. The interim dean figured out the processes for getting things changed and frequently made the necessary contacts with public schools and college administration for the pilots and program implementation.

While the SERPS was organized by departments, the organization for the redesign work evolved from the three major sets of players in the effort: faculty, administration, and consultant. The administration component included the dean, interim dean, department chairs, and the dean's assistant. (See Figure 1, Item 2.) The consultant group included the external consultant, AACTE knowledge base authors, specialists (e.g., professors in alternative, special education preparation programs at other universities), and a program evaluation consultant. The external consultant worked with the other consultants during the organization for three retreats and with the program evaluation consultant during the pilot phase of the redesign effort. (See Figure 1, Item 3.) A fourth configuration was the faculty consultant groups. (See Figure 1, Item 4.) Cross-group meetings occurred for the purposes of redesign work. For example, redesign work necessitated working with members of the consultant group, reading department, and secondary department. The dean's assistant met with the secondary program group since he was a teaching member of that program. At times he also met with the elementary group as he was concerned about cross-department program congruence. The consultant also worked with the faculty/administration configuration composed of department chairs, and, the SERPS union representatives. (See Figure 1, Item 5.) The administration/consultant group included the dean, interim dean, external consultant, and, on occasion, the evaluation consultant. (See Figure 1, Item 6.) Finally, at times, the external consultant met with all participants. (See Figure 1, Item 7.) These occasions were the initial three retreats and winter and fall work during the second year.

Faculty Conceptions, Capacity, and Efficacy

Information gathered from group discussions, observations of and discussions with student teachers, and survey data indicated that the faculty held a wide range of diverse ideas about teaching, learning, and the preparation of teachers; they also had varying viewpoints about changing their teacher preparation programs. Once again the survey data helped to inform both the consultant and faculty about the group's ideas.

The faculty's response profile, on both questionnaires, portrayed, in general, the faculty as having a wide range of perspectives. For example, diverse responses were found relative to items about what was currently happening in their program (e.g., many faculty said they believed that student analysis of videotapes of their own teaching never happened, while others thought it was happening on a regular basis). This variance raised the question as to how valid the perceptions of faculty were about the program beyond their own courses or supervision experience. Virtually no agreement existed among the faculty on their views of teaching and learning (e.g., the item, "teachers should avoid grouping students by ability or level of performance," elicited a full range of responses from "always" to "never"). The wide range of responses appeared also in response to questions about the importance of a teacher's ability to: assess and use pupil's prior knowledge, demonstrate a conceptual understanding of academic subject matter, and think critically about their own teaching. Faculty showed some agreement about what they thought was important in evaluating student knowledge and performances in courses (e.g., make logical and well-supported arguments in written work).

The same survey provided a basis for understanding faculty perspectives about themselves as a group. The survey data indicated that faculty believed that, as a group, they lacked vision and that this contributed to the primary problems restricting change. They were evenly split as to whether they believed that faculty were or were not committed to improving their teacher education programs. This lack of vision was also evident in the faculty's written reactions to the chapters they had read and processed with the authors of the KBBT volume. Responses to the information ranged from "there is nothing new here," "our students could never do these things," "this is a political statement and should be avoided," to "there is a lot we should be doing differently."

The faculty's perceptions of their efficacy as individuals, informal groups (e.g., people who teach foundations), and formal groups (e.g., as departments and as a School of Education) primarily reflected the notion that little could be done within the current state and local organizational structures. The school's organizational structures were not designed for renewal efforts (e.g., there were no study committees, regular colloquy, program evaluation, or program standards). The existing teacher education programs consisted of isolated courses with little or no connection between coursework and field performance criteria. Faculty believed they had no power and that their professional decisions were not supported by policies (e.g., they believed they had to pass all students in student teaching). In fact, however, procedures existed to handle the student-teacher problems the faculty identified and for giving incomplete or failing grades, but they were not used. Additionally, the effect of all the state-mandated changes and their implementation seemed to contribute to general feelings of low efficacy.

Initially, the consultant found it difficult to determine the faculty's capacity for qualitative change. While numerous changes had occurred on paper (e.g., there were fewer credits to teach, new course titles and outlines), no systematic revision of the programs' goals and curricula had occurred. However, since the faculty had not worked on the earlier changes, the consultant inferred that it was possible that, given the opportunity, faculty would become intellectually challenged and invested in program redesign.

CHANGE PHASE II: MOVING THE REDESIGN PROCESS ALONG

The initial three retreats provided the basis for designing a long-range change process. To move the redesign process beyond the study of the KBBT volume, the external consultant and the interim dean worked as partners to get things going. By October of the first year, the consultant took the lead in developing a conceptual framework for the redesign process. (See Figure 2.) She provided direct leadership in designing the activities for meetings at the beginning of the change process. She acted to get things started and to establish the norm of making progress through individual and group effort. Each meeting was coupled with tasks to be accomplished before the next group sessions would occur. The interim dean took the lead in organizing time and space and in carrying out communications across the school and in between the consultant's site visits. She was instrumental in "making the plan happen."

The redesign system included the recurring processes of exploring, synthesizing, and designing. Exploring provided opportunities for faculty to review their programs, read, and look for new ideas and information. Periodically the focus of the sessions was on pulling together what people were learning (synthesizing) and on determining what progress had been made and what else needed to be done. Designing was the process of creating and putting in writing the goals, substance, and procedures for new teacher education programs. The exploring and synthesizing activities were the primary processes used over the first six months and functioned as initial staff development activities. Once designing work actually began, exploring and synthesizing continued but were directed by questions emanating from the designing tasks. All redesign activities could be characterized as one of these processes. The faculty and external consultant used the exploring, synthesizing, and designing processes to keep doors open to continuous change, to focus and reduce complexity at different times, and to provide direction and products for review.

During all sessions the consultant observed and asked provocative and clarifying questions. She was challenged by others about her intent, role, knowledge, and ability to provide external leadership for the redesign effort. After one meeting a faculty member came up to her and confessed that she had said what she did during the meeting simply to see if the external consultant could handle conflict. As the consultant worked in the context, she began to share her observations about the indicators of change, reoccurring roadblocks, and actual changes in productivity.

The consultant planned activities for development sessions that would contribute to the progress of the group. When new information was needed, readings or other resources were provided for review and deliberations. For example, the consultant read program documents; the faculty asked to see course outlines from alternative programs at other universities; faculty asked to read research papers and articles, chapters related to specific program questions (e.g., classroom management and organization). The consultant worked to establish a study and investigation mode of exploration. The external consultant established the practice of making on-site visits every three weeks. Between visits faculty were asked to review their work to date and to find new questions to be processed during the impending visit. Not all groups or individuals completed each task, but over time, more faculty followed through and more was accomplished. The norm related to faculty discourse, and professional role moved from isolation and entrenchment toward one of exploration and productivity.

Once faculty became engaged in exploration, the external consultant was satisfied that the development of the faculty was in process. However, before the faculty would be able to work together to define and design a program, their capacity and trust of each other needed to be established. Additionally, it was realized that the organizational structure (capacity to manage new programs and support design work) of the institution needed to be confronted and changed.

Capacity Building

As stated earlier, the structures in place and the norms of the organization did not support the redesign of teacher preparation programs. For example, new faculty were told "not to chair meetings" and "to be quiet as they did not have tenure." Additionally, no program or evaluation standing committees were in place to support/promote redesign. The faculty also had not historically been encouraged to engage in redesign work. For example, resources for purchasing scholarly publications as evidenced in the professional library were nonexistent, turn around time for word processing requests was frequently over a month, and faculty felt that giving work to a secretary was asking a favor.

Thus, the external consultant began building capacity by working with the formal leaders to determine their commitment to the project and their ability to promote organizational changes and redistribute limited resources. Early in the process it became apparent that two levels of commitment from formal leaders for building capacity would be necessary. It would take one type of capacity to get redesigned programs on paper and yet another capacity to actually implement such programs.

Trust Building

The strategies employed in the early redesign phase focused on building trust through improving communication and building awareness of current practices. Trust was built for two context-specific purposes. First, trust was built that the consultant was there to support the faculty's decisions, not to import some program from her own institution. Trust was built among the participating faculty such that if the faculty did the work and created new programs, then neither the formal administrative leaders nor the nonparticipating and negative faculty would be able to kill their programs at the last minute. Some faculty had to develop trust that they would not be "sold down the river" and end up with yet another paper change that in reality would not make a difference. And even worse, they would have invested their time and have had their hopes for creating and sustaining an intellectually challenging environment unfulfilled.

To develop faculty trust in the consultant, the consultant adopted the role of advocate for the faculty, to support the study and further definition of "their programs." She made clear what she thought and helped faculty to build their own positions. She debated with faculty, taking multiple positions on a given issue as a means of looking at short- and long-range consequences. She called attention to decisions that faculty made during the redesign process, both to be sure that faculty were conscious of agreements reached and to clarify whether or not any one decision was congruent with prior decisions. During each site visit the interim dean asked some faculty from all departments to meet with the consultant on a one-to-one basis or in small groups, providing support for individuals to be heard and for an ever-widening basis of shared information. Once faculty met with the consultant, some asked to continue to meet about once every two visits.

To support building trust between the consultant and leadership of the School, the consultant, the dean, and the interim dean met at least twice per visit, and talked about fears, roadblocks built into the current structures, and potential support. The deans took action to support the leadership of faculty and to include increasing numbers of faculty in the redesign process.

Trusting that the organization would support changes was a major problem. For an entire year, some faculty worried that in the end, someone would not "let them" implement any plan they created. Once they started to pilot courses, this fear subsided. Attempts from some faculty to stop the change process were bothersome too. The naysayers worked to dissuade tentative faculty each step of the way. In fact, until the second summer, "problem rearing/roadblock language" was more apparent in Early Childhood and Elementary Education Department large-group meetings than was "moving forward language." However, the incidence decreased steadily from the time of the November meetings in 1988 (Karwowski & Sharp, 1990). In January 1989, the faculty reported that they could see they were getting closer to the goal. They had a week-long design session to identify the goals they wanted to accomplish in the program curriculum.

By spring 1989, faculty agreed to pilot courses during the next school year. Faculty worry about the "naysayers" had shifted to worry about whether or not formal leaders could solve practical problems, such as changing schedules for courses (planned a year earlier) and finding new field sites. The interim dean's insider knowledge of the institution and the school districts made this a short-term worry.

Developing trust on the part of new faculty who entered the redesign process along the way was another task for the external consultant. These faculty needed support as they gained entry into the working group and developed the trust of their colleagues. The consultant worked with these people to encourage their contributions and responsibility for tasks. She also helped "old-timers" handle their frustrations when new members failed to follow through by reminding them that norms had changed among those who were originally involved and that newcomers needed time to make these changes.

Organizational Support

When the faculty reviewed their current programs, they concluded that they needed to be redesigned. However, as noted above, departments were not structured to support the work, and committed faculty worried that others had the power to stop the programs from being redesigned. For example, they worried that they would invest in redesigned programs, and then others would veto them by vote in a department meeting, or that the curriculum committee would simply not support the new programs and course outlines.

Each of three programs approached the academic organization problems from a different perspective. One department sought support from the department membership early and created a redesign committee with an appointed chair. Another department worked out of the department's regularly scheduled meetings, acting as a redesign committee "of the whole." In a third department, a subset of faculty acted as a redesign committee and worked independently of the department until they had a plan to take to the department for consideration. This subset simply did the work and produced a new program design. In the cases of the first and third departments, the groups brought along the members of the departments in ways that solidified the idea of a program and helped all faculty to understand the program and the contributions of each course to the expected program outcomes. The department that acted out of the committee of the whole struggled with the tendency to perpetuate the offering of isolated courses rather than to create a coherent program structure. Their decision to hire an outside person to write up courses and submit the program through the governance system contributed to this problem. When faculty began piloting courses they finally confronted programmatic questions such as: how much content is too much in a given course; what and how much field work is needed to practice and apply what was taught; and how can redundancy of content in courses be reduced?

Program Definition and Design

The initial summer/fall retreats in 1988, at which KBBT authors spoke and faculty participated in planned deliberations, created the readiness for faculty to ask the question, "Why redesign our programs?" Initially, faculty claimed that their programs were outstanding, or that no new ideas or research had been provided during the three retreats to warrant considering the redesign of their programs, or that they really did not know what was being taught in the courses. To answer the "why" question, the consultant designed two tasks. (See Figure 2, points 2 and 3.) The first was a process to help faculty understand what they believed individually and as a group about teacher education. These activities were designed to facilitate sharing beliefs, values about teaching/learning, and what was being done in their programs. The second was an analysis task that involved consultant and faculty in the review of course outlines from current programs. The analysis took two forms. First, guidelines from various agencies important to the institution and to individuals were gathered. These were synthesized and shaped into a vertical representation that formed one arm of a matrix. The course names and numbers were used to form the other matrix. Some faculty indicated that the Boyer objectives, NCATE guidelines, and various state and professional subject matter guidelines should be reflected in their courses. Second, small working groups were given the task of reviewing each course and indicating where the specific elements were found in courses.

These tasks provided the basis for faculty to develop shared understanding of their programs and to hear what other faculty believed was possible or impossible to accomplish in a teacher education program. Opposing points of view about teacher education were identified. One view was that teacher education programs had to focus on teaching such things as rote learning and following teachers' guides verbatim. An alternative perception was that one reason public schools are in such trouble is because teacher education supports the memorization point of view. Analysis of the present teacher education program, while a frustrating event for some faculty, resulted in two understandings. (See Figure 2, Point 4.) First, formal programs were defined by outsiders rather than by the faculty themselves. The existing programs were a conglomeration of isolated courses, the content of which depended on who was teaching the section and what book was ordered. Second, programs did not have explicit goal statements; thus, there was no basis for faculty to have an explicit shared understanding about the relationship of their courses to intended outcomes.

Taken together, these two sets of activities (Figure 2, Points 3 & 4) resulted in a group of faculty being ready to pursue the redesign of their programs. The next task relative to the design process was to help faculty determine what they needed to explore additionally in order to develop new images of teacher education. (See Figure 2, Point 5.) This step provided the basis for the shift from avoidance or tolerance ("this will all pass") to a position, by a critical mass of faculty, of "let's get on with it." This shift brought the groups to the place where it was necessary to determine the direction for their design work.

To determine where each group would enter the design deliberations, the groups talked about content, outcomes, experiences, or strategies as potential starting points for program development. (See Figure 2, Point 6.) After exploring all four starting points, each of the three program groups decided to start their design work with deliberations about what their graduates would know and be able to do. Once some statement of program goals was agreed on, each group then moved to identifying the professional knowledge to be included in the program curriculum. The curriculum was then sequenced and chunked into courses. Once a sequence was determined, deliberations turned to how the curriculum would be taught and the design of clinical experiences. In general the design work occurred following this process. Each of the program groups worked as a whole to review written documents or build conceptual frameworks. Small groups were formed to work the specifics of an area once general consensus was reached. Individuals wrote up the results of small group work, which were then reviewed by all involved.

The external consultant and interim dean provided visual representations of frameworks or sequences of professional knowledge. They challenged the faculty to be explicit, to clarify their disagreements, and to carry their stated goals through the entire set of deliberations. At one time faculty from each of the program groups visited other universities. The field trips acted as energizers for the faculty. The trips also provided concrete examples of teacher education organizations, activity, and teacher candidate knowledge and performances to help faculty build a clear vision of their own program. (Figure 2, Point 7.) To this point in the process, 15 months had passed. The next phase involved piloting and revising the newly designed programs.

CHANGE PHASE III: PILOTING AND IMPLEMENTING REDESIGNED PROGRAMS

The piloting phase took 11 months and resulted in increased faculty and institutional capacity. A strategy to study the effects of the piloted courses was designed as soon as it was evident the courses would be piloted. The plans differed in each department. Carrying out and studying the pilots of formal courses and field work assignments contributed to further development of faculty expertise, administrator strategies for managing nontraditional programs, and school site capacity for handling new organizations of teacher candidates in schools. Findings from the study of the pilots were used to further refine the redesigned programs. The study of the pilots contributed to faculty's feelings of efficacy.

Developing capacity, creating conditions, and trials and study of practice and of implementation are the key elements of this phase. The programs are just being implemented as this chapter is being written. Initial observations of faculty concerning implementation are included but must be viewed as tentative.

Developing Capacity and Creating Conditions

Concurrent with the design of the programs' new curricula, the interim dean, dean, and department chairs worked to find responses to questions raised concerning how to pilot and implement the new programs. These responses included:

- changing course schedules and faculty assignments to provide for piloting courses;

- finding new schools in which to place large sets of teacher candidates for early field experiences;

160

- establishing new expectations for field work among supervisors, cooperating teachers, and principals;

- clarifying the formats and timeliness for taking the new programs through the institution's governance systems; and

- identifying organizational structures to support the continual revision and updating of the programs. (See Figure 2, Point 8.)

The external consultant kept these questions on the agendas for her meetings with the interim dean and dean. Thus, when it was time to pilot courses, the procedures to begin and to establish new expectations were in place.

Piloting courses helped create a greater capacity for change and feelings of efficacy by providing the faculty with an opportunity to identify real problems with which they would be confronted and to solve those problems while they were in the frame of mind to "experiment and try new things." Faculty found that both they and the public schools could do things that they had previously thought impossible. Faculty who were invested in keeping the status quo found their arguments against change confronted. Threats made by naysayers about what would happen when the new program was implemented were found to be empty. The pilot, in fact, helped the faculty see that they had the ability to problem-solve, that not all problems were unsolvable, and that there were even more people in the public schools and college who were supportive of the change effort.

Trials and Study of Practice

The process used for the pilots varied by program group. The most formal was that carried out by the elementary certification program. This group followed a six-step process that was open to the involvement of all the department's faculty. During the early steps in the process, the external consultant provided leadership for group deliberations. Later in the process, when the courses were piloted and being revised, the interim dean and others took more and more responsibility for group leadership and processing. The steps were as follows.

Step 1 included reaching agreement on course outlines and actually teaching the courses. In teaching the new courses, faculty ran into several problems. When faculty communicated new standards to students, they found the students expected coursework to be similar to that reported by former students, and they reacted with resentful statements indicating that they should not be expected to do more or to do different things than students in previous years. Faculty teaching the same course were uneven in their own ability to deliver it, and by the end of the semester, students began to react that they were not "getting what others were being taught."

Step 2 included the external consultant's review of written work from each section and interviews with students in the presence of the instructor. The primary question that the consultant used to focus her review and interviews was: How are assignments, written student responses, and students' verbal articulation of the professional knowledge and performances linked to stated program goals and course objectives? To help answer this question, faculty asked three members of each of their classes to participate in helping them study the effects of their new courses. They invited students they felt would best represent the range of reactions the faculty were getting in their courses. Students were told that the external consultant would look at their work and talk with them once a month. The faculty then sent the consultant copies of student work, which were reviewed and from which interview questions were developed. Once a month the students, consultant, and faculty met. Faculty and students sat in a "fish bowl" arrangement, and the consultant and students talked. Students were grouped by specific courses for these deliberations. Only faculty knew which students were in whose section.

Step 3 included deliberations among faculty teaching a specific course. Faculty met weekly to talk about instruction and reactions to their instruction, student progress, and conceptual problems that students were encountering. They called the external consultant to discuss problems, insights, and recommended changes.

Step 4 focused on deliberations among faculty teaching all the different pilot courses. In these sessions, the consultant's role was to ask questions, help raise issues, and to keep responses to problems always tentative. Throughout all discussions the consultant facilitated deliberations so that topics were considered in light of stated program goals, course objectives, or general program expectations.

For the elementary certification group, the pilot (See Figure 2, Point 9) was also the time that they began "Friday Breakfast Deliberations." One faculty member invited all of the faculty piloting courses to have breakfast at her house once every three weeks. Having faculty, administrators, and a consultant sitting around a large oval table provided the occasions for faculty to reconnect socially, to problem solve, to "get it off my chest," to challenge each other, and to provide ways to support each other.

The "Friday Occasion" also provided a way to plan short- and long-term changes. For example, change in who would teach which courses arose when two members found that their courses were suffering because of extreme differences in their styles. Thus, Friday meetings provided the opportunity for faculty to begin to verbalize, hear, and work out problems related to: things that a member of group could "not live with," social support, student responses to increased expectations, and organizational supports that were needed. It should be noted that problems of the "can't live with it" variety resolved themselves as clarity about courses and program outcomes was accomplished. Individuals who thought they would never be able to work in the same courses with others ended up as members of some of the strongest partnerships. The previous experiences in program definition and design provided the basis for new professional relationships. The new activity, "Friday Breakfasts," added a personal/professional aspect to the working group's relationships. Time invested in working on the redesign and meeting in someone's home fused to help individuals make commitments and take instructional risks that had appeared unattainable before.

Piloting was hard on the faculty for a number of reasons. Some faculty found that they were spending more time at work (on campus and in meetings, and being challenged by their colleagues). The professional program development work at the School took more hours and was requiring more intellectual engagement than the old work norm. The serenity of teaching "my" classes, attending department meetings, holding office hours, and taking care of mail was disrupted. Perhaps an even bigger problem existed for faculty who saw themselves as the professors whom students "liked." These professors found they were "in conflict" with the students over the new norms of performance and general academic standards. Because of this conflict, one professor stopped talking to the consultant for several weeks. The consultant encouraged movement forward and sticking to the course plan.

Faculty seemed to lack strategies for talking with students who were "upset" with them. Further, faculty were not used to being told negative things about "their" courses or "their" teaching. On the other hand, faculty who initially had reputations as having high standards were also confronted with the same student talk about "norms in the program." However, this group of faculty focused on improving their instruction and being more explicit with their students about what they were learning and how the learning was connected to teaching performance. They contacted the consultant by phone and talked with each other about their teaching. The consultant suggested specific course activities and responses to student comments. As the quality of their instruction increased and their activities and assignments more closely matched the stated course objectives, negative feedback from students decreased. These faculty became the "favored" faculty. Presently the unevenness of faculty and course quality has resulted in students being unhappy with "lower quality" course instruction. Both faculty and the external consultant predict this will remain a problem until all faculty are committed to facilitating the teacher candidates' learning as related to the contribution a particular course makes to the overall program.

It was not until the first part of the second semester of the pilot that faculty believed that their change effort was worth it. By the time the second semester of the pilot occurred, faculty were teaching one course they had piloted the first semester and a second new course in the sequence. They taught the new courses to students who had been in the first semester pilot. The results of their instruction during the first semester were immediately apparent. As the students began to use the knowledge taught in the first semester pilot courses in subsequent courses, the faculty saw the potential for achieving a systematic program and became invested in making the additional changes that would be needed for implementation of the program. At this point, the consultant's role shifted from one of support and providing recommendations for changes in teaching to one of challenging the faculty.

The pilot resulted in the clarification of what was needed for the new program to be implemented in each department. Faculty found that:

- pilot courses had too much content in them,

- faculty carried too many old teaching activities into the new courses that were unrelated to new expected outcomes,

- explicit field assignments and evaluation criteria throughout the programs were needed,

- standards among faculty were incongruent,

- communication was needed with field sites about what students needed to observe and do, and

▪ teacher candidates could do all sorts of things that were not previously expected. (See Figure 2, Points 7 & 8.)

The consultant helped work out specific responses to each of the above, sometimes working with groups, sometimes with individuals, but always working from their initial ideas.

Step 5 consisted of field trips. Once again the faculty visited other universities to look at their teacher preparation programs. Some faculty visited the same program they had seen a year earlier. Based on their pilot experiences, the second visit provided them with the opportunity to ask different questions and to observe university faculty, teacher candidates, and cooperating teachers from new perspectives.

Step 6 was the redesign of the new curriculum sequence and piloted courses. (See Figure 2, Point 10.) The pilot provided data that raised questions about the sequence of the content and the quantity of ideas that could be taught so that candidates would be able to use the professional knowledge in their practice. In June, the faculty rewrote their curriculum sequence and course outlines. These were submitted to the governance system. (See Figure 2, Point 11.) In August, the faculty reviewed the course outlines once again. They then worked to complete: the design of field notebooks for teacher candidates and cooperating teachers; student teacher requirements, evaluation instruments, and norms for observing and debriefing students; and written course assignments, field assignments, and exams for courses.

Implementation

The implementation of the programs began in fall 1990, 26 months from the beginning of the formal redesign effort (Figure 2, Point 12) and as this chapter was being written. Thus, questions still exist about whether the formal organizational structure can sustain the faculty's enthusiasm, continual renewal, and upgrading for quality. Some reports indicate that field supervisors who do not teach courses are unwilling to facilitate early field experience assignments or related evaluations of performances. Faculty teaching courses, however, report congruence between the students' courses and support of teachers.

A professor who participated in the original change study wrote a proposal (funded locally) to study the implementation year. This study, now in process, is focused on faculty attitudes and student outcomes. (See

▪   ▪   ▪   ▪   ▪   ▪   ▪

Figure 2, Point 13.) It should contribute to the program's evolution over time. (See Figure 2, Point 14.)

Currently, it is evident that the discourse norms of old are still a part of the culture. Some faculty believe that the external consultant should have continued to work through the first year of implementation. This would have provided faculty with the support needed to establish new norms necessary for quality program evolution.

■

EXTERNAL CONSULTANT'S COMMITMENTS AND JUDGMENTS

Creating new programs requires developing new visions, making images concrete, and trying to do new things. The doing of each of these brings with it the creation of new problems, miscommunications, and the need for new social discourse and problem-solving norms. To handle the problems, the relationships among developers need to be such that they weather the problems as they occur.

In this redesign project two major themes explain the process of relationship-building between the external consultant and the faculty. The first theme is consultant commitment to the goal of local redesign of teacher education programs. The second theme is objective judgments.

Commitment to the goal of local redesign means that the external consultant makes decisions based on the assumption that programs will be redesigned and that the redesign work will be the result of the faculty's capacity, desires, and work, and what is currently acceptable as sound educational theory and research. The second theme, objective judgments, means that the consultant uses information about the context and professional knowledge to foster the change process and sees problems as things to be resolved in the process of program redesign. For example, the consultant used assessment information to make decisions that would support the goal of locally redesigned programs, rather than using information to formulate subjective judgments about the worth or value of individuals.

■   ■   ■   ■   ■   ■   ■

Three principles at interplay during the redesign process were found to contribute to the building of relationships necessary for redesign work. These are: intensity of work, role versus personal orientation to work, and diverse representation.

INTENSITY OF WORK

The intensity of the working relationship contributed to the speed with which the core group developed trust and the increase in numbers of participating faculty. The consultant's work schedule "on site" was usually from 8 a.m. to 9 p.m. for four days every three or four weeks. The typical schedule was to meet at the beginning and end of each site visit with the dean and interim dean. Each department that was redesigning a program scheduled a half-day of working time as a group with the consultant. Individuals scheduled appointments to talk about specific redesign problems, to get feedback, and to explore ideas from the various readings that were studied. Lunches and dinners were generally working sessions. During the first year, lunch and dinner times provided informal opportunities for individuals or pairs of faculty to get to know the consultant, to discuss their redesign ideas, to talk about their fears, and, to share their perceptions about the change process. During the second year, individuals scheduled dinner meetings to work on tasks related to instruction, course assignments, or field assignments. Breakfast meetings with the consultant were added during the pilot year by the elementary department.

The consultant's work across many groups and individuals provided local faculty with an increased work and meeting schedule, but no one person had to be involved all the time. A balance had to be struck between redesign work and the maintenance of their ongoing teacher education programs. Related to this balance, several discussions occurred during the design work about the tensions regarding their own competence that faculty experienced.

CONSULTANT'S ROLE ORIENTATION

The external consultant kept in mind that her role was to facilitate the design of teacher education programs. As an external consultant she was able to ask tough questions of everyone, including herself. The questions challenged or asked for clarification about beliefs, values, assumptions, and past practices. While all external consultants can do this, a new responsibility becomes associated with asking questions when the consultant becomes an insider consultant and is part of the ongoing redesign effort. The insider consultant's membership in the groups and her continuous reappearance kept her involved in helping to answer those tough questions, as well as in asking them responsibly. The effect of this involvement was to support faculty in figuring out responses to the difficult questions. The consultant acted as a resource rather than simply a critic. Being connected and moving to "inside consultant role" insured that "tough questions" asked were timely and helpful ones for the context. The insider consultant role provided the consultant with the security that there was time to ask the critical questions, the opportunity to lead and work with the people involved, and the responsibility to challenge and provide necessary support so that progress occurred.

The consultant had no vested interest in a particular program curriculum or outcome, as her role was to help faculty create "their own" program. Her job was to help faculty keep, at a conscious level, what was currently thought to be sound educational practice in the area of teacher preparation and learning to teach; to ask questions relative to applications of standards from professional organizations; and to help them define, pilot, and implement their ideas. Thus, the consultant did not insist that any set of recommendations be followed but questioned why they would or would not be considered and, ultimately, why they were discarded or accepted.

The nature of the work that the consultant did over the two-year period included a wide range of tasks, such as: challenging assumptions and practices, supporting conflict, encouraging risks, soothing impatient and fed-up leaders, synthesizing position papers, creating representations of abstract ideas generated by faculty development groups, and giving feedback on written work. The consultant did not do the redesign work for the faculty groups. She acted as a member of groups who were struggling with the problems and questions. (Given that the context was different from that of her home institution, these were also real problems for her.) She had to work them through with the faculty. She had no preconceived answers. This reinforced the consultant role as an inside consultant and the local faculty as the owners of the program.

Providing conceptual frameworks based on group deliberations appeared to promote progress; at times when groups were stuck, the consultant proposed conceptual organizational structures. Faculty also proposed conceptual and procedural structures as the process moved along and the structure of the new programs became clearer. Further, the consultant worked with individuals to support their work with others. Perhaps most challenging was helping faculty to identify roadblocks and see them as problems to solve rather than as personal attacks.

The consultant provided challenge and support for both faculty and administrators. Consultant characteristics identified by the dean as crucial to the success of program redesign effort included:

- knowledge about program redesign, educational theory, research, K-12 teaching and learning, and teacher preparation;

- interpersonal skills relative to assertiveness, acceptance, flexibility, and congruence;

- goal orientation; and

- experience in the field of teacher education, program curriculum design, and university level staff development work.

In most cases the role is not unlike that of a hockey coach (Duffy, 1990). Hockey coaches do not teach players plays. Instead they help them figure out how to see their environment and use it to accomplish the goal.

DIVERSE REPRESENTATION

Redesign relationships need to support the valuing of diverse ideas, including diverse intellectual contributions and perspectives from a variety of people. Valuing diverse contributions is critical to the design of a new program if faculty are to develop ownership and if the new program is to reflect their conceptions of teaching, learning, and learning to teach. Redesigning programs brings with it the "threat" to the status quo and disruption of the comfort of faculty and administrators. As discussed earlier, trust and respect are necessary in order to progress through the period of time that the redesign takes.

Even with unconditional trust and respect among most participants, problems will inevitably occur. In reality, some structure of trust and respect relative to the redesign period will need to be established. In the case described in this chapter, unconditional trust and respect were developed only among the external consultant and a subset of the total redesign group. The interim dean played a major role in initially getting a diverse set of faculty to spend individual time (e.g., eat lunch or dinner) with the consultant. This provided contact with a diverse set of faculty, and it resulted in opportunities for the consultant to learn about the wide range of perspectives held in the School. The same results may not have occurred if the interim dean's effort to diversify contacts had not been made. One outcome of exposing diverse faculty to the consultant was to encourage participation of more faculty members. When the consultant was not trusted by a given faculty member, however, some other member of the core development team served a similar function.

The relationships among the core group grew over time and resulted in a number of faculty communicating directly and frequently with the consultant. They telephoned and wrote between site visits. They invited the consultant to conferences and to participate in writing papers and preparing presentations. The consultant moved from visitor consultant to an external consultant to an inside consultant. She remained a consultant in the sense that she never became vested in the particular program they designed or in local politics. The consultant frequently talked about "being adopted by some of the School's faculty" during the redesign process. She observed that now when she attends national conferences, she is treated as a valued colleague by a wide range of "local site" faculty.

For the consultant, the experience provided insights about four key factors in a change process. A primary factor was the need to understand the context. This meant that she needed to get to know the faculty, their strengths and capacities, who stuck with things and followed through, and who could be counted on for what. She also needed to understand what local politics existed, what administrators could and would support, what the nature of support and challenge to faculty consultant and administrators would be, and what level of change would be possible in a given length of time. For example, after the consultant had worked with the faculty for about four months, she realized that by summer 1989, it might be possible for the departments to have new programs on paper. Whether or not faculty would ever implement the programs was a question that was dependent on change in the environment and the capacity of individual faculty.

Understanding the people and institution from the consultant's perspective was only one part of the understandings that had to be developed. A related factor, and equally important, was developing an understanding of the context from the perspective of the local faculty. This included not only uncovering their ideas about why things were as they were, but also what change might be worthwhile and probable. As the process unfolded the consultant kept in mind that what was being learned had to be interpreted from the perspectives of the faculty members themselves. That is, whatever is happening is being experienced by the faculty in ways that may differ significantly from that of the consultant. Understanding the faculty's interpretations helps with plans for developing effective working groups and assessing progress.

A second factor that became apparent to the consultant was the need to build a professional community. This need is even more evident today, as the programs are in their first semester of implementation, than it was during the pilot. During the redesign work the external consultant's role reinforced and supported a professional community. The professional community norms that were initiated contributed to the successful design and piloting of programs. For example, during tense deliberations, the consultant acted to keep conversation open when someone acted to set up roadblocks to progress. She would offer multiple suggestions, raise new questions, and illustrate different responses to a given problem. Another contribution to the professional community was her role in helping to find solutions and actions that suited a wide variety of people.

A third factor was the importance of effective leadership among faculty and administrators. From the consultant's perspective, faculty and administrator leaders are critical to initiating, advancing, and carrying out change. Neither faculty nor administrators can carry out redesign work alone. The importance of having shared visions and support for the redesign cannot be overstated.

A fourth important factor was the capacity to accommodate ambiguity and error. The increase in stress on the institutional structures and individuals must be expected. Feelings related to survival appear to be dependent on members trusting the knowledge, motives, and skills of others, as well as having faith in their own capacities. While risk to individuals seemed to diminish as goals were identified and individuals begin to make commitments, tension for the system is likely to continue well beyond initial program implementation.

■

FURTHER QUESTIONS

Program redesign with the use of a consultant in a leadership role raises many questions. Among these are: Was all of this necessary as part of the change process? What is the nature of the relationships among people that are needed for change? What is the best balance to strike between interpersonal relationships and distance? What site-specific circumstances could alter the external consultant's role? As the process of redesign is undertaken in other institutions, answers to these and related questions may emerge.

■

REFERENCES

Barnes, H. (1989). MSU Exxon Project Report. East Lansing: Michigan State University College of Education.

Duffy, G. (1990, Nov.). *What counts in teacher education: Dilemmas in educating Empowered teachers.* Presidential address delivered at the 40th annual meeting of the National Reading Conference, Miami Beach, FL.

Karwowski, L., & Sharp, C. (1990, Fall). Section IV: A case study of change in our department. *Education, 111*(1), 26-36.

Putnam, J. (1990, Fall). Section III: Program redesign and design phases. *Education, 111*(1), 15-26.

Rilling, M. (1990, Fall). Section I: Forces for change, and Section II: An oral history: Thinking and planning. *Education, 111*(1), 6-14.

Rilling, M., Sharp, C., Karwowski, L., & Putnam, J. (1990, Fall). Emerging knowledge base in teacher education and faculty renewal and program redesign at Glassboro (NJ) State College. *Education, 111*(1), 5-42.

■ ■ ■ ■ ■ ■ ■

CASE THREE: CHANGE THROUGH COMPREHENSIVE DELIBERATION IN A LARGE, MULTIPURPOSE INSTITUTION

8

HENRIETTA L. BARNES

Overview. While the goal of the preceding chapter was to engage faculty within a single unit of the university in reforming the professional studies component of a teacher education program, this chapter describes efforts to engender institutional support across several units of a large university. The approach described in this case was designed to build support by allowing faculty within every department that contributed to the education of teachers to have input at several stages of the redesign process. The approach was based on the premise that support for the program would be more likely if the resulting design contained elements of the diverse perspectives and interests of different faculty groups across campus. Through analysis of the tensions and frustrations that accompany such collaboration, questions are raised concerning the limits of shared understandings for reconciling fundamental differences in view of competing reform agendas. Although deliberations were often seen as uncomfortable and frustrating, the educative value of having open discussions about the education of teachers is highlighted as critical to improving the status of teacher education on university campuses. ■

■ ■ ■ ■ ■ ■ ■ ■ ■

When components of a teacher education program are the responsibility of different departments of the university, dialogue across these departments about the purposes and goals of the total program is traditionally nonexistent. Yet, deliberation about the conception of the teacher that guides the selection of essential content should be consistent across the different elements, if the student's preparation to teach is to be experienced as coherent. Creating a forum within which common understandings can be shaped is a challenging enterprise. But the task is essential if comprehensive change in the total program is to be accomplished.

As part of its attempt to reform its teacher education program, one of the 11 institutions in the Michigan State University Exxon project addressed this problem through the approach described here. This case describes how one institution structured opportunities for discussions that involved representative faculty and administrators from across the university, and teachers and administrators from the public schools. These deliberations spanned one academic year and culminated in proposals that are currently undergoing further refinement and negotiation in preparation for academic governance review. The inclusive approach used brought into focus the diverse perspectives held by different groups about teaching and teacher education, and highlighted the tensions that have historically made comprehensive change of the total teacher education program problematic. This case description discusses those tensions, and ways that the original proposal is being modified to respond to the diverse interests of all participants.

Deliberation around issues of teacher education reform occurred at several levels, and included a variety of participants over time. Figure 1 illustrates the groups that were organized to deliberate about the redesign of the teacher education program. Faculty within the Department of Teacher Education began the discussions in 1986-87. Small faculty groups were formed at that time to consider the criticisms and calls for reform of teacher education that were part of the national debate about the quality of teaching and teacher education.

In spring 1987, the advisory committee of the Department of Teacher Education invited the advisory groups of the other departments in the college to join them in initiating a proposal for pursuing these ideas on a collegewide basis. The proposal was drafted in the form of a resolution and was submitted to the College Council, a body comprising faculty representatives from each department, the department chairs, and chairs of each of the standing committees within the College of Education for discussion. The College Council then established a task force with membership carefully planned to include faculty from

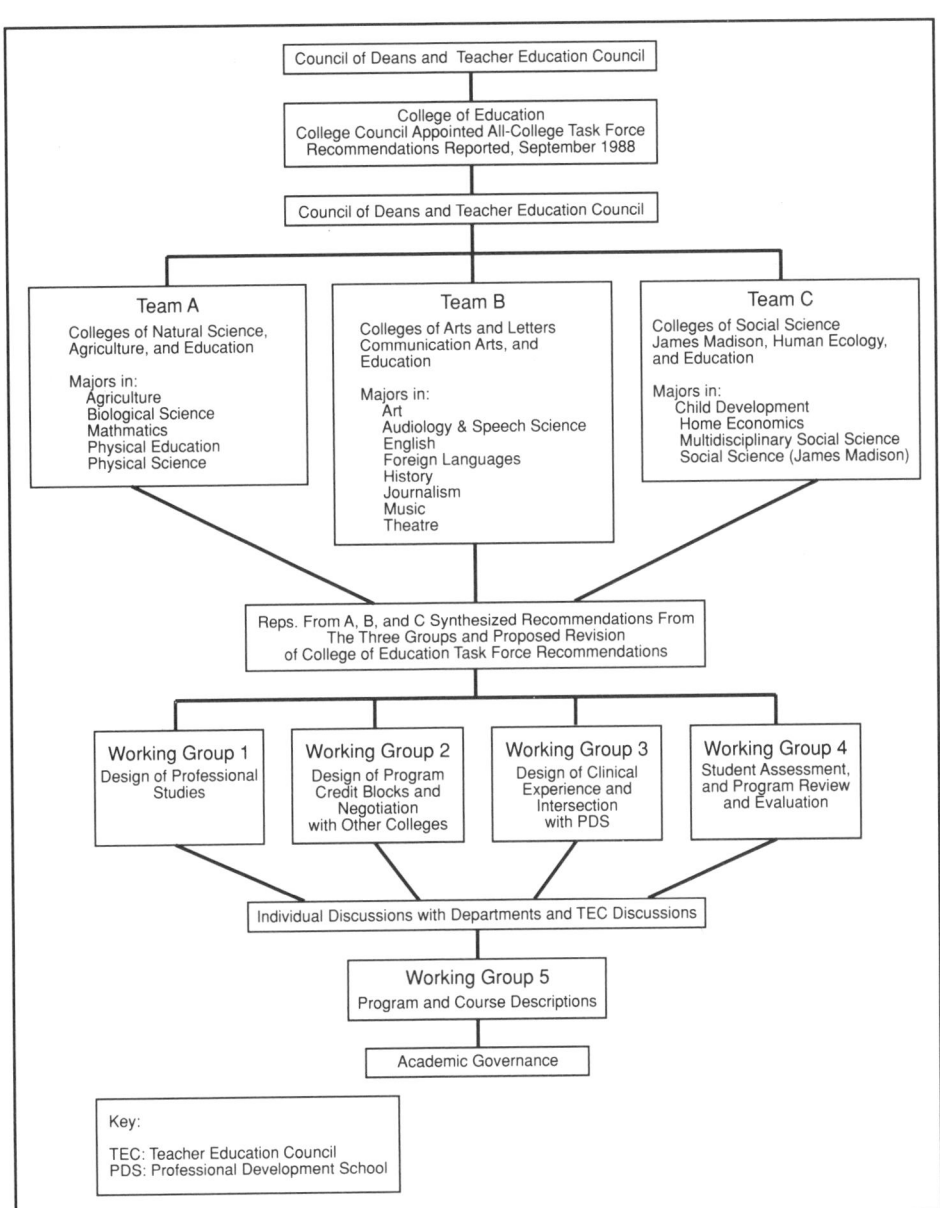

Figure 1. Deliberative Process

all departments of the college. That group met across the span of one year and hammered out goals for improving the existing program. Further, the task force outlined strategies for communicating with others in departments that were providing general education courses and specialty area studies for teacher candidates, to test the validity of the stated goals and to develop consensus concerning ways to achieve these goals with students.

The goal of extending the conversation held a purpose beyond wanting to establish dialogue among those faculty and administrators who shared some responsibility for the teacher education program and, thus, were stakeholders in the enterprise. Support from faculty and administrators across the several departments of the university was seen as essential. It was assumed that such support could be built through reasoned deliberations and that faculty across the campus would come to share ownership for whatever proposals eventually would be submitted through academic governance.

Creating a structure within which to develop support and ownership, and selecting participants were in themselves difficult tasks. Deciding how to begin such a conversation was complicated because of the diversity of backgounds and interests of various stakeholders. The organization that was established to carry on these discussions was based on the assumption that faculty from the arts and sciences would be more likely to see the discussions as relevant and worthy of their time investment if they felt that the outcomes of the deliberations would directly affect students majoring in their departments. Thus, it was reasoned, it would make sense to organize discussions by disciplinary areas. In contrast to this view, however, was the argument that while schools require teachers who can teach the various subject matters, schools also need teachers who understand conditions that extend beyond the teaching of those subjects as they work with learners, parents, communities, and social agencies. Organizing groups that paralleled the professional workplace, therefore, would bring cross-disciplinary perspectives to the discussion of problems of educating youth.

Furthermore, the forum would be more likely to achieve its goals if participants entered into discussions in good faith, willing to share their points of view openly, to weigh arguments for and against different positions, and to come to reasoned conclusions about what could be done collectively to ensure that prospective teachers were well educated and prepared to engage in professional work. On the one hand, the effort could quickly become a shambles if participants chose to use the forum to argue their own perspectives uncritically. It was assumed that participating in this kind of dialogue would be more comfortable within faculty groups who had some common experiences and perspective, and from whom individual faculty could expect support as well as challenge. Thus, it was concluded, participants should be grouped so that the discussion could center on students from related fields that had a common disciplinary base. This arrangement would allow faculty to focus on the students with whom they were familiar, but would force them to generalize to students beyond their majors.

In the end, it was determined that these considerations should be accommodated within teams that brought faculty from related disciplines together, with faculty that represented different approaches to educational dilemmas. Then to ensure that cross-disciplinary perspectives were represented, participants from all of the departments of the college of education with backgrounds in social, philosophical, and psychological foundation areas, mathematics, science, literacy, social studies, history, and clinical studies were included on each team. Based on this rationale, three teams were formed:

- one with primary participation from the Colleges of Natural Sciences and Agriculture that included faculty from mathematics and various science areas, agriculture, and physical education;

- one with the Colleges of Arts and Letters and Communication Arts that included English, history, foreign languages, art, music, audiology and speech sciences, and journalism; and

- one with the Colleges of Social Sciences and Human Ecology that brought together faculty from the various social sciences, early childhood education, and home economics education.

Resistance to the idea of such comprehensive deliberation showed itself almost immediately. While deans of the various colleges supported the idea that the institution should join the Holmes Group, and although they had been kept informed throughout earlier discussions, they expressed concern that they had not given formal approval for the College of Education's recommendations. When the proposal to engage in deliberation about these ideas was first discussed with department chairs and selected faculty, some deans wondered if they were being bypassed and asked that faculty be appointed through their offices. Other deans preferred that a College of Education representative contact department chairs, and still others were comfortable with faculty being contacted directly.

On later reflection, it was clear that many of the tensions felt initially within the teams arose from the ambiguity of the situation. While the recommendations of the College of Education task force were used as a springboard for discussions, teams were encouraged not to let these ideas constrain their consideration of other promising directions. The task force report had focused on four primary goals that this group wanted for all graduates of the teacher education program and had recommended continuation of program features that ensure articulation and program coherence. Specifically, the program should:

- instill deep understanding of subject matter disciplines and related content specific pegagogy;

- inculcate a deep commitment to equitable access for all children to valuable, empowering knowledge, and develop the capacity of graduates to work with children having special educational needs;

- equip graduates to establish "learning communities" in their classrooms and schools, in order to realize the goals of academic learning and social justice; and

- instill professional norms that would improve graduates' engagement in the profession, decision-making, and practice in the future.

In addition, the College of Education task force had recommended that professional and clinical study be integrated with study of the major field within a liberal baccalaureate degree program, with certification coming at the end of a master's degree that included an extensive internship around extended professional roles for teachers. A specific proposal for program credit blocks and courses had not yet been drafted. Since the College of Education faculty wanted such a proposal to reflect the broad interests of the university community, the idea was to talk about what was needed and possible ways to respond to those needs collectively. The actual design of the curriculum and ways that it would be delivered were to be accomplished through later developmental work. The College of Education had proposed deliberation about ideas, and wanted both reaction to the proposals and suggestions from other stakeholders on other ways to proceed. The teams were asked to consider these recommendations, generate others, and come to some agreement that could shape the final plans.

In hindsight, the planners might have anticipated the difficulty inherent in talking, at a conceptual level, about ideas that, if adopted, would strongly affect the work of the discussants. Political and resource questions were raised repeatedly. Faculty expressed their unwillingness to spend time talking about visions that might not come to fruition. They saw time spent in this way as a waste of valuable energies. Some wanted assurance that whatever they came up with would be implemented without change. Others had difficulty imagining how teacher education could be done differently because no additional resources had been promised. Still others saw the political difficulties of trying to change the structure and nature of the teacher education program and felt powerless to confront these realities.

Other tensions stemmed from very different perceptions among participants about what teachers need to know and be able to do, in order to begin to teach. Faculty across all units had strong beliefs about what prospective teachers should and should not study, and what they could and could not learn. The preparation of elementary teachers is a case in point. The proposal for elementary education students to have a regular academic major was not universally embraced by faculty as a good idea. While most saw the need for elementary teachers to have deeper understandings of the subjects they teach, they questioned the feasibility of such a requirement. For some, the idea of an academic major for elementary candidates seemed ludicrous because they did not accept the premise that elementary teachers need to know a great deal more about the content they would be teaching than is actually taught in the elementary curriculum. According to this view, preparation to teach a subject to small children requires knowing little more than introductory level coursework in the various areas. Others saw the requirement for an academic major as foolish because they believed that aspiring elementary teachers would not be able to pass the courses required of a "regular" major. Despite the fact that the current all-university grade point average for students admitted to the elementary education program is as high as that of students accepted by disciplinary departments for their majors, the perception that these students are unable to succeed in rigorous programs persists among some faculty in the arts and sciences.

Despite these dissenting views, however, most team participants supported the recommendation for stronger preparation in the academic disciplines that undergird elementary school teaching. What that preparation should include, however, was another matter for debate. Some contended that elementary teachers, like their secondary counterparts, should major in a single academic discipline. This argument was supported by the contention that intensive study of one field can empower teachers to understand other disciplinary fields. In addition, it was argued, in-depth understanding in one field would make apparent the advantages to teachers of having such knowledge, and would encourage them to continue their learning in other fields after they completed the preparation program. Others asserted that special majors should be constructed for elementary teachers. These majors should be as intellectually rigorous as traditional disciplinary majors in academic departments, but might be designed to expose prospective elementary teachers to a range of intellectual territory that would prepare them more broadly for teaching all the subjects in the elementary school. The concern of primary importance to these advocates was that these majors would not consist of strings of introductory courses, but would be sets of courses that exposed students to the fundamental ideas of the discipline in ways appropriate for their career goals.

Discussions about what constituted an appropriate undergraduate major raised other important questions for all teacher education students, secondary as well as elementary, about knowledge and whether or not knowledge of one area can generalize more broadly to other areas. One set of arguments was based on the conjecture that teachers need to be liberally educated individuals and, thus, should be allowed to major in any field they wish to pursue. This position was supported by the reasoning stated above that held that students who come to know how knowledge in a particular discipline is generated, validated, and organized can effectively help their students develop such understandings in other fields. The counter-argument was based on the view that there are particular majors that have so little connection with the subject matter taught in elementary and secondary schools that students should be encouraged to major in a select number of academic disciplines. The goal of undergraduate and graduate teacher education, it was argued, was not only that teachers come to understand disciplinary knowledge in general, but that they understand deeply the particular disciplines they will teach.

Deliberations about the substance of pedagogical studies were also controversial. The view that education courses have no substance, and the accompanying assumption that there is, in fact, nothing of substance to teach in such courses was not often articulated. Nevertheless, discussions often revealed the skepticism that some faculty had concerning both the need for more intensive pedagogical study and questions about the nature of such content. Despite position papers written to explicate the rationale for providing stronger connections between a student's disciplinary study and the pedagogy for teaching school subjects for understanding, and the need for greater integration of these knowledge areas with knowledge about diverse learners and multiple contexts, these views remained basically unchanged throughout the deliberations.

On the one hand, faculty across all groups agreed with the need for teachers to be sensitive to diverse learners, capable of becoming advocates for all learners, and able to confront injustice where they encounter it in educational and community settings. On the other hand, they did not always recognize the legitimacy of such knowledge for teacher education. While faculty did not disagree with the statistics that point to grave difficulties confronting teachers in some settings, they also did not see the study of these contexts as critical to teaching. For some, these issues are the domain of study for policy makers and administrators, but not for teachers. Others would ignore these factors on the grounds that they influence learning little, if at all, and therefore should only be touched on briefly in education courses, but require little more. Similar questions were raised about the importance of understanding the diversity which learners bring into the classroom. In the end, however, it was not so much that the proposed content was not recognized as important, but that faculty did not agree about how teachers can learn what they need to know.

Perceptions about how individuals learn to teach tended to be more consistent among faculty within the College of Education than across college affiliations. Faculty in the College of Education generally accepted the idea that teacher candidates had to construct understandings, both of teaching as presently exists, and of ways that the practice of teaching could be different. They believed that the entering assumptions, attitudes, and conceptions of teaching that aspiring teachers hold must be made visible, so that alternative conceptions of teaching, learning, learners, and schools could be considered. Faculty in the College of Education embraced the notion that important, but different ways of understanding teaching and learning must be accommodated within a coherent framework of knowledge domains. They believed, further, that the opportunity to develop these understandings must be thoughtfully constructed, using a variety of materials and experiences. They recognized that such learning requires coherent programming and an extended time frame.

These assumptions were not generally shared by faculty in other departments. While other faculty saw the same needs being demonstrated by their students, they tended to interpret these needs as deficits in the students' academic preparation (i.e., too few courses in the disciplines) rather than as problems stemming from too little integration of disciplinary study with the study of teaching, learners, and schools. Thus, solutions proposed by such faculty generally focused on ways to include more content in the major fields, rather than on ways to deepen both disciplinary and pedagogical understandings. Such recommendations on content were also justified on the grounds that novices should be expected to learn to teach "on the job." Given this premise, the primary purpose of the university program would be to expose students to knowledge that might be useful, either as an orientation to the demands of their future teaching roles, or as ideas they might later use as teachers. Helping novices create networks of understanding that bridge theory and practice was not completely accepted by faculty on these teams. Thus, tensions about both the appropriate substance and the duration of the professional studies component continued throughout the yearlong deliberations.

In addition to the debates mentioned above, three primary concerns surfaced early and persisted throughout the year. One of these concerns focused on discussions of the advantages and disadvantages of proposing certification at the end of a master's degree program. Another had to do with a desire, on the part of other colleges, to include disciplinary study across both the baccalaureate and master's degree components of the program. Still another had to do with the advisability of completing a master's degree in the absence of full-time teaching experience. Discussion of these and related issues led to modifications in the overall design of the integrated BA/MA program; these continue to be further refined and negotiated individually with forum participants and the administrators of the various departments that provide specialty area studies for prospective teachers. Proposed modifications include:

- exploring the feasibility of a dual emphasis on both disciplinary study and professional study at the BA level, with continued study of the disciplines along with professional studies at the MA level;

- considering a model that provides provisional certification at the end of the fifth year of study; and

- pursuing the possibility of including the induction year as part of the master's degree program, thus providing support for first-year teachers and allowing candidates to meet a substantial portion of their continuing certification requirements as part of the program. This proposal assumes that special education content will be merged with general education content within the professional studies component of the program.

■

CONCLUSION

The decision to engage in long-term discussions across all departments of the university that contribute to the preparation of teachers was grounded in the belief that only through understanding of the common agenda could the institution hope to achieve its goal of improved teacher education. While such a forum can foster some understanding, it is unlikely to be successful with all participants. Thus, many of those who took part in these discussions remained unconvinced.

The deliberative approach just described revealed many of the tensions and difficulties inherent in institutional change. Yet, the process was useful for accomplishing some important purposes. While some participants appeared reluctant to alter their current practices, others took the opportunity to build more collaborative approaches to teacher education. Although some were unwilling to accept basic premises of the reform agenda, they did participate in discussions and present alternative points of view.

The primary value of the deliberative approach, however, lies in its educative function. Through this forum, faculty and some administrators (department chairs and assistant or associate deans) engaged in regular conversations about the educational needs of the nation's youth. Faculty considered new views of learning and teaching and delved into the dilemmas confronting teachers in different contexts. This year was an opportunity to examine their own values and perspectives on the role of various kinds of knowledge in teaching and learning to teach. Faculty from all departments had opportunities to influence the perceptions and goals of faculty from departments with whom they had had virtually no prior contact. Together they shared perspectives and contemplated strategies for achieving the broad goals they each held.

While some teams were more successful than others in achieving some consensus within the team, differences persisted across teams in the priorities that different groups identified. Some teams were clearly more focused on the importance of strong subject matter preparation, while others placed somewhat more emphasis on developing understandings of learners, contexts, and social justice issues. As an educative device, however, this forum

■　■　■　■　■　■　■　■

highlighted education as an important and worthwhile commitment of the university. It was also worthwhile as a vehicle for identifying ways to modify the proposal to gain the support needed for formal university approval.

Inasmuch as the process is not yet completed, the jury is still out concerning the final outcomes of these deliberations. Three things are clear, however:

- there is more consensus about what is needed than there is about what should be done about these needs,

- talking about these issues uncovered promising possibilities to pursue as well as sore spots to avoid, and

- knowing who one's likely allies are provides the possibility of developing broad faculty ownership of the ideas. These realizations are important since the academic governance system relies on political support from all colleges for proposed curricular changes. Knowing where such support already exists, and where other support can be built is invaluable for the success of proposals for change.

Building such support is particularly important in universities where teacher education is considered an all-university responsibility. The sort of support that is needed, however, requires that faculty work together over time, as they educate students with whom they have continuing relationships. Next steps, therefore, include plans for cross-disciplinary faculty to form faculty cohorts that will enact the curriculum that is ultimately negotiated through the academic governance system of the university. As these cohorts collectively plan and implement strategies that foster the conceptual understandings and teaching competence of their mutual students, faculty are likely to further refine and develop shared conceptions of teacher education that they can fully support.

Unless university faculty and administrators come to embrace common goals, and develop proposals that they can participate in fully, the aim of creating comprehensive reform will not be realized. Yet, creating a forum for the sharing of ideas is frustrating, difficult, and politically dicey. Nonetheless, it is essential that such dialogue occur if teacher education is to become an important mission of the university. The approach described here is one way to begin the conversation.

CASE FOUR: BUILDING ON FACULTY COMMITMENT IN A SMALL LIBERAL ARTS COLLEGE

9

SHIRLEY RICHNER

Overview. Contexts of institutions vary enormously. Where existing communication patterns are relatively open and conversations across departmental units are ongoing, efforts to reform teacher education can evolve rather easily. Building on positive attitudes and faculty relationships, renewed commitments to teacher education may be adopted readily with little or no dissension. The case description that follows illustrates the advances that were possible within the context of a small liberal arts college. In contrast to the difficulties associated with cross-departmental deliberations described in Chapter 8, it is tempting to speculate that the important distinction to note between these two cases is the size of the institution. On the contrary, change within a small institution may be equally or even more difficult if faculty are not supportive of proposed changes. A single dissenting voice can carry great weight when faculty numbers are small. When faculty trust and support one another, on the other hand, these qualities become instrumental in accomplishing proposed reforms. ■

. . . .

Liberal arts colleges have a long history of involvement in teacher education. Some of this involvement has developed because of the desire of private religious colleges to prepare teachers for their related K-12 private schools. But the tie between liberal arts and teacher education is much broader than the preparation of teachers for specific schools. The emphasis on liberal arts that is at the heart of the mission statements of most private colleges leads logically to the additional mission of preparing the teachers who will contribute liberal education at all grade levels and in both public and private schools. Whitworth College, a private, residential, liberal arts college located in Spokane, Washington, is an example of this traditional partnership between liberal arts and teacher education.

The development of the *Knowledge Base for the Beginning Teacher* volume by the American Association of Colleges for Teacher Education (AACTE) provided the impetus for study and change for the teacher education programs at Whitworth College. The purpose of the two-year project at Whitworth was to implement changes in the knowledge base used in the preparation program for beginning teachers. This project included an in-depth study of the recommendations made by the authors of the KBBT volume. These recommendations were compared to the knowledge base in use in the department's existing program. With this knowledge as a reference point, Whitworth's education faculty made decisions about the importance of the knowledge contained in the KBBT volume, and in existing courses in relation to the conceptual framework which was developed for Whitworth's program. These decisions led to the implementation of changes in courses and programs.

■

INSTITUTIONAL CONTEXT FOR CHANGE

Before this project began, teacher education programs at Whitworth were generally considered successful. Graduates of the program were in demand by school districts and evaluations of first-year teachers showed a high degree of satisfaction with the current program. Because the current programs were viewed as successful, there was a difference in the degree of faculty members' perceptions of the need for change to be brought about through the project. It is always harder to "fix" things that are not broken. To broaden faculty support for the project, the task was approached as a professional growth and renewal effort.

From the start, the faculty of the education department had a shared vision for teacher education. The programs were "owned" by the department as a whole, and the expectations for faculty were high. There was a long history of working together in a consensus model. The number of people in the department was small enough for total involvement, but large enough to have diverse ideas and interaction. The ten full-time faculty members had the basic responsibility for change. Their preparation represented expertise and experience in elementary, secondary, special education (including gifted education), multicultural, educational foundations, evaluation, and liberal arts disciplines. Some of the people had taught in the department for more than two decades; others only a few years.

In addition to the advantage of size, the department faculty genuinely liked each other and cared about the personal and professional success of the other members. No one hesitated to say what they thought, yet all were kind to each other. The working relationship of this group of people was an important part of the context for change.

The Education Department is the largest department of the college. More than 20% of the graduates who receive their B.A. degrees each year have also obtained their teaching certificates. Between 120 and 160 students receive their initial teaching certification each year.

Another important factor in the institutional context was the close working relationship among the education faculty and the faculty of the other college departments. Whitworth's Education department and content departments have historically viewed themselves as partners in teacher education with joint responsibility for the success of beginning teachers. The faculty in the content areas model good teaching and participate in the selection process for students seeking to enter the teaching profession. Education faculty serve on the teaching teams for the core program and act as resources for college-wide faculty development. Achieving this working relationship has been a twenty-year project. It has required constant attention as faculty and programs changed.

Teaching excellence is also a characteristic of the education experience at Whitworth. Outstanding teaching is a prerequisite for both tenure and promotion throughout the institution. This historic priority for good teaching creates an atmosphere in which the study of teaching is valued.

Another important component of the context for change at Whitworth was the positive and supportive attitude of the institution's administrators. The college encourages creativity and change, and administrators provide support for departments that wish to implement changes. Changes are easier to make when decisions and approvals are all made at the institution. A private college like Whitworth does not face the more complex decision-making process that most public institutions have.

These factors created an institutional climate that was very supportive of initiating and implementing change in the teacher preparation program at Whitworth. Unlike many larger, comprehensive institutions, the college did not face such obstacles as low prestige accorded to teacher education, lack of administrative support for the costs and process of instituting change, problems with collaboration across departments, or a slow-moving bureaucratic structure for implementing new programs. The absence of such obstacles allowed the college to proceed at a rapid pace and with a high degree of consensus in developing the new program for teacher preparation.

NATIONAL AND STATE CONTEXT FOR CHANGE

The state of Washington responded in very direct fashion to the series of national reports in the mid-1980s that called for reform in K-12 education and teacher education. A comprehensive study, commissioned by the State Superintendent of Public Instruction, concluded that teacher education in the state of Washington, was "not at risk." An example of evidence leading to this conclusion is the fact that almost all of the state's teacher education programs were NCATE accredited. But, despite this evidence of healthy professional preparation, the national reform movement swept across the state anyway.

At Whitworth, the effect of these national studies was to increase the amount of time that faculty and administrators within the Education Department had to spend with those outside the department to keep them informed about the quality of teacher education at our institution. The erroneous assumption that the information contained in these reports was true of Whitworth's programs had to be corrected with the entire campus community.

The NCATE redesign had a more positive influence on change. Whitworth College valued its long-term NCATE accreditation, and was willing to invest time and resources to meet the new stricter standards. Whitworth viewed the knowledge base standards as the central focus of the new NCATE standards as well as the ideal starting place for implementing changes in courses and programs. Therefore, faculty deliberation about knowledge base issues became the initial focus of the change effort and a central element of this project.

Some of the new state requirements played a major role in creating the framework for Whitworth's change process. One component of the governor's program was the provision to offer, for the first time in the state, initial certification programs at the graduate level. These programs were designed to attract qualified people with B.A. degrees in liberal arts subjects into the teaching profession. The development of the Master in Teaching program leading to initial certification was a major part of the change process at Whitworth. The requirement for all teachers to have Master's degrees before continuing certification was also included in this legislation. This requirement led to changes in advanced programs for experienced teachers as well as reconceptualized programs for beginning teachers.

The other major factor at the state level was the revision of the program approval standards and certification requirements. The new state standards, which are similar to the NCATE standards, are designed to avoid duplication. Like the new NCATE standards, the revised state standards require institutions to base the components of the professional preparation program on a "theoretically sound and research-based framework." The state standards also seek assurance that the education unit has "established procedures for the review of such theory and research regularly, and has made a commitment to revise the professional preparation program on the basis of evaluation of the program and relevant new knowledge in the field." The need to meet such standards obviously gave impetus to the Whitworth knowledge base implementation project.

The office of the State Superintendent for Public Instruction had a history of supporting creativity and change in teacher education. The state has established teacher education advisory boards, beginning teacher assistance programs, and a number of other innovative programs. Institutions are encouraged to go beyond basic standards in the development of their programs. The state's requirements, for the most part, are broad and leave room for the faculty at each institution to develop creative professional programs.

The overall context in which Whitworth undertook to re-examine and revise its approach to teacher preparation was a positive one. While national reform proposals and new state requirements placed the teacher education program under increased scrutiny and accountability, there was also clear guidance on the general objectives for change and an encouragement of innovation within the state. The supportive environment at the institution level allowed the Education Department to utilize these external factors as facilitators for the change process.

■

PROCESS OF CHANGE
IN TEACHER EDUCATION PROGRAMS
AT WHITWORTH COLLEGE

Change efforts at Whitworth used the KBBT volume as a point of departure for responding to the state's mandates for redesigning teacher education programs. The faculty of the Education Department specifically chose to concentrate their efforts on the knowledge base for a number of reasons. They included:

1. The department's belief that the specialized knowledge for teacher education should be central to the program and that all courses and decisions should be made in relationship to it.

2. The increased emphasis on the importance of the knowledge base for beginning teachers in the new NCATE standards and in the new Washington State certification standards.

3. Whitworth College's emphasis on departmental study and change.

4. The department's need to revise the conceptual framework of its programs and to ensure that the most recent research and theory were being used in all of its courses and programs.

5. The department's desire for each faculty member to have a better understanding of the total program and of the place of each of their courses in the program.

■   ■   ■   ■   ■   ■   ■   ■   ■

6. The department's desire for clearer and more direct relationships between the courses and the conceptual framework and improved communication of these relationships to students.

Additionally, two crucial elements allowed this effort to move forward. One was the leadership role of AACTE in organizing developmental projects on the professional knowledge base for beginning teachers. The other factor was the financial support provided by an external grant with which the project was initiated.

Actual changes in teacher education programs could occur only if the ten faculty members of the Education Department initiated, developed, and implemented these changes. For this to happen, the faculty needed to spend large blocks of time together. A series of one- and two-day retreats was planned. Classes were cancelled and faculty were paid a small stipend for retreats that extended into the weekend.

The agenda for the first retreat was an in-depth study of the knowledge bases of the current program, with special attention to the strengths and weaknesses of each content area. This close look at the knowledge base for teacher education programs seemed like a logical place to begin because of the perceived success of those programs and because of each faculty member's personal and professional investment in each of those courses. Beginning here, however, tended to strengthen the status quo, and make changes more difficult.

The next step was for each faculty member to review the material from the KBBT volume. This was organized according to the teaching areas of each faculty member. The department had to work from manuscripts as they became available because much of the change process occurred before the book was published. At first this was experienced as a major handicap. But it forced the faculty to assume the primary role in the development of its own programs, and allowed the book to be a source rather than a blueprint. In retrospect, the timing of the book seemed to be an advantage rather than a handicap. It became available *after* the department was asking all of the right questions.

Each faculty member had to incorporate the new knowledge that the profession believed to be important with what he or she already knew and believed about teaching. The next retreats then dealt with the comparison of this recommended knowledge base with the knowledge already in use in each of the courses.

The department continued to meet in its regular two hour sessions in the time between the retreats. Although other business had to be conducted during these meetings, at least a part of the time was devoted to continuing the knowledge base discussions. This kept the project at the forefront of the department's work throughout the two-year period of the change process.

An outside consultant met with the department at one of the early retreats to discuss the change process. This consultant helped the department see the need for revising and developing the conceptual framework for the beginning teacher program, and for relating each of the program components to this framework. She also challenged some of the department's current thinking and practice and suggested directions and sources which would prove basic to the changes that were actually made.

DEVELOPING A CONCEPTUAL FRAMEWORK

The next step for the department was to develop the conceptual framework. This was a difficult part of the process, and progress occurred only after some decisions were made about knowledge base priorities. When the department was dealing with both areas simultaneously—knowledge base priorities and conceptual framework—they were able to make progress. The addition of new sources and knowledge, and the reaffirmation of some current knowledge, generated new ideas about the overall conceptual framework. During these early meetings, several faculty members who were on the cutting edge of professional knowledge served as important mentors for younger and older faculty. Their knowledge and enthusiasm kept the department interested and energized.

Teacher education programs in the state of Washington have advisory councils composed of teachers and administrators from public schools in the area. The council which works with Whitworth's teacher education program was advisory to the total change process. The council participated in some of the retreats and meetings and met with the consultants. The council knew the college's current programs well, and was willing to work closely with the faculty throughout the change process.

The department also received assistance from five other area colleges that were involved in the knowledge base change process at their own institutions. The department chairs from these five institutions met regularly to compare their procedures and progress. Because these institutions were regional, there was little expense involved in the meetings. The institutions were both small and large, public and private, and were located in large cities and small towns. The variety of these institutions and of the procedures each of them used helped to give perspective and support.

The department chair benefitted from the collaboration gained as a member of AACTE's Knowledge Base Committee during the two years of the change process. Since the other institutions represented on this committee were also involved in related projects with their own institutions, this committee was able to provide perspective, support, and new ideas for procedures.

SMALL GROUP TASK STRUCTURE

The next step in the change procedure was the formation of small groups to work on specific areas of the program. The idea of using small groups to accomplish tasks was new to the department. Because only ten people are involved in the total unit, the norm was for everyone to be involved in everything. Small groups were established in four areas: elementary education, secondary education, foundations, and special education. Part-time faculty and practitioners were added to these groups. The productivity of the small groups convinced everyone that better work could be done by fewer people—as long as the total group was in charge of the "master plan." A trust developed within each of the small groups, over time and, a respect for the work of the groups became evident in the department retreats and meetings.

During the period when the groups were developing their recommendations for departmental actions, the advisory council members joined the small groups for an intensive discussion. The addition of these people was an important part of the change process, and many of the eventual changes were suggested in this session.

At the same time the department was working on the knowledge base for professional education, it also redesigned the requirements for endorsements in each of the content areas. Faculty from each of the subject area departments worked with the education faculty on these revisions. These cross-disciplinary faculty groups also revised the methods courses in the content areas which are taught within these departments.

As decisions were made about changes, other program options began to develop. As they did, additional groups were formed to work out the details of the proposed option and to present it to the Education Department. The most important option to develop during the change process was the Master in Teaching degree. This program for beginning teachers would provide graduate professional education leading to certification for people who already had B.A. degrees. The decision was made to develop this new certification program in addition to the undergraduate certification program. The procedure for working on the graduate program was different because this was a totally new program and required institutional action as well as departmental action.

A committee of four faculty members was appointed by the Professional Learning Council of the college to assist the Education Department in the development of this new graduate degree. These faculty represented the following departments: English, physical education, communications, and art. These faculty members met with faculty from the education department to work on the knowledge base and all degree requirements for this alternative route to certification, which is new in the state of Washington. Progress reports were made to the graduate school, the Professional Learning Council, college administrators, the education department, and the Board of Trustees. Final approval was obtained from each of these groups.

Another knowledge source originally developed with the graduate degree in mind also became an influence on the conceptual base for the undergraduate program. As a part of the grant that funded the knowledge base change process, a research project was conducted to study the knowledge base of experienced teachers who were selected as experts by their peers. As the study of these teachers (Michaelis, 1989) progressed, it became clear that there were implications for undergraduate as well as graduate programs. Certain knowledge, skills, and models were more appropriate for preservice programs, and these were presented to the Education Department for consideration.

Throughout the process of program reform, communication was very important. The retreats and meetings required thorough and immediate follow-up action so that the next steps could be done. This became especially crucial after the small groups began to meet, and the entire department needed to be informed about their progress. The department chair and the chairs of the small groups were responsible for writing and distributing minutes of the meetings and for taking the actions recommended by the groups or the department.

■

THE CHALLENGE OF REAL CHANGE

During the department retreats and meetings, faculty members were not defensive about their courses or the status quo of the current programs. Everyone was willing to consider the sources of knowledge that were basic to current programs and to entertain the suggestions made in the KBBT volume and its associated references. But problems began to surface when the process reached the next stage. Although the faculty had created the new program and had agreed to implement the appropriate changes in their courses, it was difficult for them to actually go into the classroom and teach a familiar course differently. This factor was the most difficult one encountered in the change process at Whitworth. People agreed about the changes that needed to happen; each person intended for it to happen, but at first, it didn't.

After the unity of the group and the excitement about the group decisions, it was discouraging and puzzling to find that although the minutes of the meetings and retreats looked good, the same old courses, using the same old sources, were being taught. An analysis of the situation led to the conclusion that lack of time was the major factor in the barrier to change. Lack of time was not an easy obstacle to overcome, but at least it was easier to handle than overt resistance to change.

Other colleges involved in reconceptualizing the teacher education knowledge base with Whitworth were also experiencing this problem. One of the methods that helped faculty members implement changes in their courses was for them to attend intensive, structured conferences with faculty members who taught a similar course in other colleges. These meetings were set up to include two course areas—for example, educational psychology and methods. The first part of the meeting would involve methods professors meeting with each other and psychology professors meeting with each other. Then, as the meetings progressed, everyone met together to find ways to integrate the learning from one area with that from the other. Faculty returned from these meetings with new ideas and enthusiasm for specific changes in their courses.

To encourage change in courses, the department chair met individually with each faculty member to discuss implementation of the changes agreed on by the department. For some, there was a need to establish

■ ■ ■ ■ ■ ■ ■ ■ ■

timelines for change cooperatively. For others, these meetings provided the opportunity to discuss professional decisions related to the courses. The long-honored right of each faculty member to teach courses based only on their own professional judgment was gradually surrendered for the privilege of having a part in making decisions for the total program. New course outlines were developed that were specifically related to the conceptual framework. Faculty began to refer directly to the knowledge base as a part of the rationale for each unit of the course. The faculty who were first to implement new courses became models for others. Course outlines were shared and individuals helped each other make changes. The department chair also modeled changes in the courses she taught.

SUPPORTING THE CHANGE PROCESS

The most important support for the changes came from the faculty of the Education Department. Their positive attitude and good working relationships were of key importance to the entire process.

Support for the process also came from the college administration. There was support for released time for faculty, as well as provisions for additional funding. The Vice President for Academic Affairs took a personal interest in the changes and attended presentations and meetings throughout the two-year project.

In addition, a $48,000 grant of outside funding bought released time for the department chair and others to arrange the retreats and meetings, to see that the decisions made by the groups were carried out, and to organize and coordinate the activities of the advisory council and cluster college group. After the funding was expended, the department continued to implement and evaluate the knowledge base changes.

While the changes might have occurred in the absence of financial support, it is unlikely that the process would have unfolded in the same way. The financial resources allowed faculty to utilize ongoing opportunities to engage in the deliberation process focused on the knowledge base, on the development of a conceptual framework, and on the relationship of courses to that framework. While the state mandate required a response, support for this project allowed the faculty to use the mandate as an occasion for substantial reform.

■

THE RESULTS OF CHANGE EFFORTS

The faculty at Whitworth spent two years reflecting, revising, and creating a new basis for teacher education programs. As a result of these ongoing efforts, they implemented a number of changes. The development of a revised conceptual framework for teacher education programs was one of the changes that occurred at Whitworth as a result of this knowledge base project. This framework became the department's guide to the other changes that occurred in programs and courses. While many frameworks had been suggested and developed during the early stages of the project, it was from the small group work that the final framework developed. This uses Shulman's four categories of the teacher's role (learner, knower, guardian, and member) and develops these in the context of the beliefs and values of Whitworth College.

A knowledge base was established for the preparation programs for beginning teachers. This knowledge base blends the recommendations in the KBBT volume and the knowledge base components that have made Whitworth's programs unique in the past. Guidelines of specialty groups were also used as applicable. The faculty members responsible for each of the courses in the program have selected areas of the program knowledge base for inclusion in their courses. This base became the essential guide to changes in individual courses.

Each course was changed significantly to be sure that the essential knowledge for each area was included. Faculty members are clear about the relationship of the course they are teaching to the conceptual framework of the program. This relationship is also explained to students, so that students are continuously aware of the program as a whole, as well as of the purpose of each class. Changes occurred in the content of all departmental courses. In many courses, methods also changed as faculty began to model instructional strategies that were consistent with the conceptual framework they had adopted.

■ ■ ■ ■ ■ ■ ■ ■ ■

A new course, designed and added to the program, provides the content component of the multicultural field experience that is required of all certification candidates. This course meets weekly for six weeks prior to the month the students spend in another cultural setting; it also meets weekly for six weeks after the students return. The course is staffed by two Education Department faculty. One of these teachers is Native American and has continuing experience teaching children in tribal schools. The other has traveled internationally and worked with children's programs in Asian countries. A faculty member from the history department and a local high school teacher who is in charge of teaching immigrant children complete the teaching team for this new course.

All of the content endorsement areas were revised. The state requires all teachers to have at least two endorsement areas and recently revised the academic content required for these endorsements. The faculty of each of the content areas and the faculty of the Education Department agreed on desirable as well as required changes in the endorsement areas, and they separated the endorsement sequences from college minors for students not seeking certification. These new endorsements are now printed in the college catalog and are in effect.

A graduate program, the Master in Teaching Degree, which leads to initial certification, was developed and implemented as part of this project. Although there have been five-year undergraduate programs in Washington State in the past, this is the first time a graduate program for initial certification has been available in the state. This degree provides an intensive 15-month program for students who hold B.A. degrees in liberal arts subjects and who wish to obtain elementary or secondary certification. The first group of students completed the program at the end of the 1990 summer term, and the second group of students is currently enrolled in the program.

Because these graduate students are beginning teachers, this program uses the same conceptual framework developed for the undergraduates. But the program and the courses differ in ways that are appropriate for graduate students. Specifically, as a part of the Master in Teaching degree, a new core course was developed. Such core courses have long been a part of undergraduate degrees at Whitworth. They are interdisciplinary and focus on topics rather than on single academic subjects. They are team taught by faculty from various departments. Implementing the knowledge base for the Master in Teaching program led to establishing a core course for Whitworth's graduate programs as well. The topic for this course is "Milestones in Education: Issues and Beliefs." It combines the history and philosophy of education with a broad liberal arts perspective. It is taught by a team of faculty who have expertise in the history of European education, English and American literature, and American educational history and philosophy.

The department has undertaken this work in response to new state requirements for a master's degree as prerequisite to final certification. This requirement ensures that, for the first time, formal education for all teachers in the state will continue into the first year of teaching. The research study on the knowledge base of expert teachers done by Michaelis (1989), one of the Education Department's full-time faculty members, was completed during the two-year period of change. A knowledge base for experienced teachers can now be developed, and the study of expert teachers will be used as one component of this development. With the exception of the Master in Teaching program, knowledge bases for graduate programs have not been completed or implemented, but the department has begun to work on them.

The department also began a collection of research studies and other information that forms the basis of Whitworth's new programs. Annotated bibliographies of the information sources that the department believes to be most important are continuously added to this professional departmental file.

Changes in programs for beginning and experienced teachers were an important outcome of this effort. Equally important was the fact that this project resulted in a more knowledgeable faculty working together in more productive and creative ways. A group of people working intensely on a project of this magnitude experienced changes in themselves, as well as in the programs they revised and created. There was a significant increase in the professional knowledge of each of the faculty members. Everyone studied the new sources recommended in the KBBT volume, and everyone reviewed the sources on which previous programs were based. Because this project was action-oriented, the faculty learned much more than they would have in more traditional faculty development programs. For some faculty, the learning involved in this project added an advanced theoretical perspective to their experience.

In addition to the changes that occurred in each faculty member, important changes also took place in the way in which faculty work together. Even though the department faculty had a history of good working relationships prior to the project, they learned to be more productive during this process. They learned to stay on task for longer periods and to stay with the big projects until they were satisfied with them—for example, reaching consensus about the conceptual framework for beginning teachers. Faculty learned to trust the work of smaller groups so that things did not have to be redone in the larger group.

As a result of the two years spent in the development and implementation of the conceptual framework for the knowledge base, the Whitworth College Education Department learned that change is difficult and exhausting. This period of change was both exciting and frightening—often at the same time. At this point, the department and the college have the satisfaction of knowing that significant improvements have been made in its programs.

Whitworth College's experience with this effort was realized in the larger context of creating new teacher education programs in liberal arts colleges – programs that can meet the challenges of this decade without losing the unique traditions of their rich heritages. It was especially rewarding to be part of this change process at Whitworth College because the faculty was able to take a program already considered successful, build on its strengths, and create a new conceptual base for the program's objectives.

REFERENCES

Michaelis, R. (1989). *Study of expert elementary teachers.* Unpublished manuscript, Whitworth College, Spokane, WA.

Reynolds, M. C. (Ed.). (1989). *Knowledge base for the beginning teacher.* Oxford, England: Pergamon.

EPILOGUE

MARLEEN C. PUGACH

Changing the practice of teacher education is not easy work, but clearly such change is crucial to improving the quality of education in the United States. This volume has tried to present a realistic picture of the problems and challenges involved in changing how teacher education is carried out. The purpose of our realism is not to dissuade those who face the daunting task of reform, but rather to encourage our colleagues that reform is in fact possible, and to inform them that in many institutions the process has begun. Further, these places can serve as examples and share how it feels to undergo the shifts that will be necessary to reach our common goals.

One problem associated with the challenge of changing teacher education is accepting the magnitude of the task and recognizing that the process will be slower than we might wish. The work we embark on is not limited to how we do business within schools, colleges, and departments of teacher education, nor is it restricted simply to integrating the information in the *Knowledge Base for Beginning Teacher* volume. Rather, multiple efforts across multiple stakeholders are needed. Some of these efforts must focus on the quality of education that precedes professional preparation, namely, efforts with our colleagues in the liberal arts and sciences. Other efforts must include working in close partnership with practitioners to raise the quality of clinical sites, by integrating school improvement with the development of highly skilled, professional teachers in the schools. Yet others must deal squarely with the content of professional preparation, giving major consideration to what the knowledge base for beginning teaching is, and how best to ensure that students draw on it well as they prepare to teach in today's schools.

These multiple goals signify that, although there may be different entry points into the process of change, all aspects must be addressed, and most likely they need to be addressed simultaneously. Perhaps more important, these interrelated goals signify that both the content and the process of teacher education need attention, and that guidance and support in each of these aspects of change is warranted. In the process of reforming teacher education, substantial reform in any one of the areas presented in this volume is to be acknowledged as a milestone. Change is incremental and must be recognized as such.

Simultaneously, however, the larger goal must always be kept at the forefront to provide the framework for each change that is accomplished, and to ensure that conceptual, programmatic integrity is honored throughout the process. This means striking a continual balance between the work on specific parts of teacher education reform and the whole that such reform is meant to create. The challenge to reforming teacher education is fundamentally a comprehensive one, and the comprehensive picture developed by a group of faculty members must always be the driving force for change.

In other words, discrete tasks will not in themselves add up to changing the practice of teacher education, but engaging in these discrete tasks that take time and great energy will pay off in contributing to the whole of reform. Opportunities must be provided for faculty members to pursue developmental work internally in their schools and colleges of education, in terms of the conception of the knowledge base they adopt. As many of the chapters in this volume suggest, this task not only will involve a consideration of research-based knowledge, some of which is codified in the KBBT volume, but also will extend far beyond the volume to include a consideration of issues such as the role of practice in the knowledge base or the means by which we prepare teachers to work with multiracial and multilingual students. Other opportunities must bring together faculty members in the liberal arts with their colleagues in teacher education to engage in reforming how liberal arts education is conceptualized for those who would teach and to initiate the developmental work needed to effect such change. Yet another opportunity must focus on knowledge derived from practice, and on the kinds of field settings that would best support the acquisition of such knowledge for teachers. Each of these tasks demands attention and requires pilot work and subsequent evaluation. It is from the interplay of each of these prior efforts, within a sound conceptual framework, that the practice of teacher education can be transformed to meet the challenges of teaching in the century to come.

We have not attempted in this volume to present a single model, or "perfect" program of teacher education. Rather, we have based our work on the assumption that institutional characteristics shape and influence what can be accomplished at any particular point in time. These idiosyncratic characteristics, these local particulars, will determine which tasks are undertaken in which order, and with which players. At the same time, however, such idiosyncracies should not become a foil for reform, and past practice, however entrenched, should not be interpreted as an absolute impediment to change. Instead, the particular circumstances of each program of teacher education constitute a local context, a unique challenge for change. The four case studies related here provide a sense of how different each effort can be, and illustrate that, even in the most traditional and apparently entrenched programs, reform can be accomplished.

Reforming teacher education is a labor-intensive task, and the commitment to such change requires an understanding and acceptance of the time and effort that will be needed to accomplish this goal. Fortunately, the effort does not have to be undertaken in isolation. Implicitly, many of the chapters in this volume deal with the concept of community: a community of teacher educators developing a defensible base of knowledge, a community of learners among university faculty and school practitioners, a community of learners among preservice students themselves, and a community of university-wide scholars concerned with the preparation of teachers as an integrated effort engaging arts and sciences with professional education. The concept of community is likewise central to changing the practice of teacher education because it is the community that provides both the opportunity for reflection and the support needed to carry out this labor-intensive commitment.

At this point in the history of teacher education, we believe that another community needs to be recognized, namely, the community of teacher educators who are taking on the task of changing the practice of teacher education. With this volume, we hope to contribute to a sustained sense of community among those who are engaged in redesigning teacher education, to the recognition that the effort is not isolated, and to an understanding that the base of dependable support is growing. We hope the experiences reflected in these chapters provide new enthusiasm and direction to those in the midst of reform. To those who have not yet embarked on the task of changing teacher education, we hope this volume is a catalyst for initiating substantive, comprehensive efforts within and among individual institutions. ∎

Appendix A

ABOUT THE AUTHORS
AND PROJECTS
IN THIS VOLUME

AUTHOR AFFILIATIONS

Henrietta L. Barnes, Michigan State University

Leonard C. Beckum, City College, City University of New York (now at Duke
      University)

Richard G. Fox, University of Wisconsin-Milwaukee

Ofelia Garcia, City College, City University of New York

William E. Gardner, University of Minnesota

Isabell Horend, City College, City University of New York

David G. Imig, American Association of Colleges for Teacher Education

Brenda H. Leake, University of Wisconsin-Milwaukee

Eric Lord, Polytechnic of the Southbank, London, U.K.

Frank B. Murray, University of Delaware

Ricardo Otheguy, City College, City University of New York

Suzanne H. Pasch, University of Wisconsin-Milwaukee

Pauline Perry, Polytechnic of the Southbank, London, U.K.

Marleen C. Pugach, University of Wisconsin-Milwaukee

Joyce Putnam, Michigan State University

Shirley Richner, Whitworth College

Brigitte Rollett, University of Vienna, Austria

Arlene Zimny, City College, City University of New York

■

PROJECT SUMMARIES

1. MICHIGAN STATE UNIVERSITY

PROJECT DIRECTOR: HENRIETTA L. BARNES

The project was designed to address these central questions:

- What do beginning teachers need to know?

- How do they need to know it?

- How is what they need to know different from what experienced teachers know?

- What are the implications for teacher education of taking the knowledge bases seriously; for example, what would be included in initial and continuing teacher education programs?

- What changes will institutions need to make if their programs are to reflect these concepts?

Project activities involved three phases. In the first phase, discussions were conducted between authors of the *Knowledge Base for the Beginning Teacher* and experienced teachers, with discussion centered on the first three questions listed above. The second phase was based on conferences held with representatives of several institutions engaged in serious reform of teacher education; these discussions focused on the set of original questions, their implications for change in teacher education programs, strategies for program redesign, and institutional obstacles to change. The third phase of this project was centered at Michigan State University, where an interdisciplinary approach was developed in order to address these questions, possible changes indicated for design of teacher preparation, and institutional strategies to bring about needed changes.

■

2. WHITWORTH COLLEGE

PROJECT DIRECTOR: SHIRLEY RICHNER
RESEARCH ASSISTANT: RANDY MICHAELIS

The Whitworth project utilized collaboration between the cluster institutions for two major project objectives. In the first of these, the institutions engaged in study of the knowledge base foundations of their current programs and met with consultants to promote this study. The institutions worked to identify obstacles to implementing specific program revisions and used collaborative conferences to facilitate such change across the institutions. The discussions of program change were also linked to new state requirements for teacher education.

Whitworth College served as the center of the change effort; its teacher preparation programs were subjected to comprehensive study by faculty across the institution and to substantial redesign by the teacher education faculty. An ancillary segment of the Whitworth project was a study of the knowledge base foundation that characterizes expert teachers. Results from this study yielded information to be utilized in the continuing redesign of advanced teacher education programs at Whitworth.

3. UNIVERSITY OF DELAWARE

PROJECT DIRECTOR: FRANK B. MURRAY

The Delaware project addressed the academic preparation of elementary teachers; its objective was to develop, implement, and evaluate a new model for the six academic areas commonly taught in elementary schools. The cluster institutions were members of the Mid-Atlantic Regional Education Consortium.

The project resulted in development of several alternative approaches to the preparation of elementary teachers; most are interdisciplinary in nature and are based on distinct perspectives from which subject matter taught at the elementary level can be conceived and understood by teachers. The approaches presented combine both the subject matter commonly taught in the elementary school and essential foundation materials from each knowledge domain.

4. UNIVERSITY OF MINNESOTA

PROJECT DIRECTOR: WILLIAM E. GARDNER

The Minnesota project focused on the generic pedagogical knowledge base for secondary level teachers. It centered on two basic questions:

- What constitutes the generic pedagogical knowledge base for secondary teachers?
- How do teacher education programs achieve a professionally sound confluence of content knowledge, pedagogical knowledge, and knowledge of learners and instruction?

These questions were studied with a particular interest in the assessment of students who enter teacher preparation at a post-baccalaureate level. The project involved teams of institutions from the cluster in these activities:

- review and analysis of relevant literature,
- development of "models" that provide preparation in the generic secondary knowledge base, and
- piloting and evaluation of models in several teacher education programs.

5. UNIVERSITY OF WISCONSIN-MILWAUKEE

PROJECT DIRECTOR: SAM J. YARGER

The University of Wisconsin-Milwaukee project centered on an inquiry concerning the knowledge needed by teachers of diverse student populations in relation to the knowledge base as set forth in the *Knowledge Base for Beginning Teacher* publication. In particular, this project addressed the question of the knowledge base in the context of implications for urban teacher education programs and the necessity for prospective teachers to address the needs of all student populations. The project included two general classes of activities: faculty study groups on topics addressed in the KBBT volume, and faculty/practitioner meetings focused on knowledge and experience needed in the preparation of teachers who will work with diverse students.

6. CITY COLLEGE, CUNY

PROJECT DIRECTOR: LEONARD C. BECKUM

The goal of this project was the identification of the knowledge base successful teachers in K-12 schools believe made them successful in multicultural, multilingual urban settings. Successful teachers in K-12 schools in New York City, London, and Vienna, through self-report techniques identified the skills, techniques, and knowledge they used with their students. The analysis identified common elements in these teachers' descriptions that constitute their knowledge base.

Appendix B

AACTE COMMITTEE ON THE PROFESSIONAL KNOWLEDGE BASE 1986 – 1988

William E. Gardner *(Chair)*, Dean, College of Education, University of Minnesota, Minneapolis, MN 55455

Henrietta L. Barnes, Chair, Department of Teacher Education, Michigan State University, East Lansing, MI 48824

Leonard C. Beckum, Dean, School of Education, City College, City University of New York, New York, NY 10031*

Gary A. Griffin, Dean, College of Education, University of Illinois at Chicago, Chicago, IL 60680**

Judson Hixson, Director, Professional Development, North Central Regional Educational Laboratories, 295 Emroy Ave., Elmhurst, IL 60126

Frank B. Murray, Dean, College of Education, University of Delaware, Newark, DE 19716

Maynard C. Reynolds, Professor, Special Education Programs, University of Minnesota, Minneapolis, MN 55455

Shirley Richner, Chair, Education Department, Whitworth College, Spokane, WA 99251

Sam J. Yarger, Dean, School of Education, University of Wisconsin-Milwaukee, Milwaukee, WI 53201

---

* Dr. Beckum is now University Vice President and Vice Provost, Duke University, Durham, NC 27706

** Dr. Griffin is now Professor, College of Education, University of Arizona, Tucson, AZ 86721